JAMES ROBERTSON JUSTICE
"WHAT'S THE BLEEDING TIME?" A BIOGRAPHY

By James Hogg

with Robert Sellers and Howard Watson

Tomahawk *Press*

First published in 2008 by
Tomahawk Press
PO Box 1236
Sheffield S11 7XU
England

www.tomahawkpress.com

ISBN-10: 0-9531926-7-9
ISBN-13: 978-0-9531926-7-0

Edited by Bruce Sachs
Designed by Steve Kirkham – Tree Frog Communication 01245 445377

Printed in the EU by Gutenberg Press Limited on environmentally friendly paper.

Picture Credits
Many pictures in this book are owned and supplied by the author, © James Hogg. In other cases copyright is retained by the original owners. If we have inadvertently published a photograph without credit, please contact the publishers so that the omission can be corrected in the next printing.

Back cover illustration by Sir Peter Scott and used with the permission of Lady Philippa Scott.

A percentage of any profits made from this book will be donated to the Wildfowl & Wetlands Trust.

A catalogue record for this book is available from the British Library.

For Indra

ACKNOWLEDGEMENTS

The authors would like to thank

HRH The Duke of Edinburgh
Richard Gordon
Helen Courtney-Lewis
Howard Ferguson
John Loft and Tony James at The British
Falconers Club
Ken Annakin
Michael Winner
The Estate of Phillip Glasier
The Estate of Anthony Wysard
Pinewood Studios
Charlie Miller
Bruce Sachs at Tomahawk Press
Steve Kirkham at Tree Frog Communication
Richard Todd OBE
Stanley Baxter
Matthew Bell
Michael Craig
The late Betty E. Box OBE
Peter Rogers
Audrey Skinner
Colin Waters
Roy & Mary McKie
Mike Farmer
Mike Codd
Jeremy Thomas
Bill Sumner at Beckenham Rugby Club
Gareth Roberts at The British Comedy Society
Sir Donald Sinden OBE
Roger Upton

Graham Downing
Lady Philippa Scott
Roderick Bromley
Christopher Neame
Morris Bright
Hugh Torrens
Dominic le Foe at The Players Theatre
John Pulford at Brooklands Museum
Jeremy Rivers-Fletcher at Rivers Fletcher
Motor Racing
Dave Drummond at *Pleasures of Past Times*
Jonathan Dalrymple-Smith
Carol Davies
Mark and Pamela Fenton
Catriona Leslie
Brian Rivas
Jon Justice
Joan Bakewell
Keith Shakleton
Susan Trew
Gyles Brandreth
Lord Steel of Aikwood
Sally Smith
Chas House
Conti-Press
Volker Reiss at Staatsarchiv Hamburg

Special thanks must go to Stephen Frank for Birichen Moor, red deer and Grouse Whisky. Jamie Thomson for bagpipes, advice and ideas. And to Mr. Martin Leslie, for his inexhaustible support and unique handwriting.

FOREWORD

BALMORAL CASTLE

James Robertson Justice was a large man, with a personality to match. His extraordinary life has been crying out for a biographer. I congratulate the author for taking on the task of recounting a story that is often stranger than fiction.

Adventurer, man of many actions, naturalist, intellectual and incidental film actor, he lived every bit of his life more than to the full, and gave his friends endless pleasure and entertainment. When you have read this book, I think you will agree that he richly deserves the title 'eccentric'.

Odd as it may seem, I am not altogether sure when I first met James Justice. It was either at a cricket match at Windsor, when he had been recruited to play by Michael Parker, who at that time was my Private Secretary; or it was at Slimbridge, when I paid an early visit to Peter Scott's Wildfowl Trust. Whichever it was, he made an instant and indelible impression. However, it was only after he had bought the house at Spinningdale that I got to know him and Irina at all well. His passion for hawking – and spearing flounders in the nearby Fleet estuary – was infectious; activities that were thoroughly enjoyed by my two older children.

I can only advise readers to be prepared to be surprised.

H.R.H. The Duke of Edinburgh

INTRODUCTION:
"YOU – WHAT'S THE BLEEDING TIME?"

With these immortal words, James Robertson Justice confirmed his place in the post-war British comedy pantheon in his masterful role as St Swithin's consultant surgeon, Sir Lancelot Spratt, in 1954's classic film *Doctor in the House*. As an actor, he appeared on stage (although just the once), radio and television but his greatest achievement was in the cinema, at home and abroad. He worked with many of the great film directors of the twentieth century, such as Alexander Mackendrick, Howard Hawks and John Huston. Not to mention the acting talents of Gregory Peck, Katherine Hepburn, Bob Hope and, of course, Dirk Bogarde.

His success in the cinema always mystified Justice, but he was aware of the freedom that it gave him to pursue his varied other interests. He liked to describe himself not as an actor but as a naturalist and truly hated it, indeed would switch off faster than light during a conversation, and be extremely rude even, when people called him a film-star. He always thought of himself as a Natural Scientist.

Justice was one of those Falstaffian figures – portly, bold, rumbustious and cheeky, who emerge from time to time from obscurity to become a legend whilst still alive. With his stentorian tones, allied to a tall and imposing frame, Justice was the quintessential authority figure in dozens of British films, after the years of austerity and before the advance of the consumer society. His bark was usually worse than his bite, he was a reassuring figure to the audiences that flocked to witness him in supporting roles throughout the fifties and sixties; he often stole a film from under the nose of its star. As summed up by Dirk Bogarde's character, Dr Simon Sparrow, in *Doctor at Large* (1957), he was "a bit of a bear."

James Robertson Justice led a full and active life. He was a brilliant raconteur, who fathered many tales but was a warm and generous host. His interests were manifold including fast cars, women, food and drink. A keen collector of jade (he once spent his entire fee for a film on a much desired jade piece he'd seen in an antiques shop)[1], wildfowler and naturalist are but three of the guises that Justice adopted throughout his extraordinary life. Twice Rector of Edinburgh University, traditionally a position little more than a figurehead, he became an advocate for the students. A committed socialist and ardent royalist, he was a man of varied tastes, deep interests and huge contradictions. He saw action too, in the Navy during the Second World War and before that volunteering to fight with the International Brigade against General Franco's fascists during the Spanish Civil War.

But his greatest legacy must be as a falconer. His knowledge of the sport embraced its ancient past, but he was also a lover of the thrills and spills of practical hawking in the modern age. He was a keen ornithologist and conservationist, too and often stressed that he acted in order to finance his interest and love of nature. Justice used to tell friends that the film business was something he got into by accident and the only way he'd ever discovered where he could work for six months and earn enough to keep him in the style to which he liked to be accustomed for the other six months. When it had been suggested to him that there had to be something about the acting profession that he liked, Justice replied, "The emoluments aren't exactly to be sneezed at."[2]

Friends and colleagues recognised that Justice on the big screen was the same man they knew in real life. Yet there were many sides to his larger than life personality, genuine accomplishments and an equal number of elaborate masks – some that will be revealed in this book, others to be discovered and some that may never come to light. He had a film career that spanned over a quarter of a century and was dedicated mostly to comedy, like the universally popular *Doctor* films. But adventure pictures too such as *The Story of Robin Hood & His Merry Men*, *The Guns of Navarone* and *Scott of the Antarctic* featured his talents. His life away from the studio was, incredibly, even more dramatic.

---

[1] Author interview with Betty E Box – Pinewood Studios – July 1994

[2] Interview with Joan Bakewell – BBC Television – 1966 – last shown in 2004 as part of BBC4's 1960's season.

CHAPTER 1:
ABSENT FATHERS

James Robertson Justice was a man who never much worried about the truth if it got in the way of a rattling good story. He even fibbed about his own birth, insisting his whole life that he'd been born in Scotland, not at 39 Baring Road, Lee, South London, which was in fact the reality. His family then moved to Bromley in Kent. For much of his life Justice considered Scotland his spiritual home. When he sailed from Liverpool for Canada in 1929, intending to emigrate, he gave his nationality as British but his people as Scottish[1], and he bought numerous properties in the country, residing there in contented heaven. He was also the proud wearer of the kilt and the Robertson tartan.

Justice knew that his family's roots were firmly north of the border, but his later adoption of the Robertson moniker (he'd in fact been born James Norval Harold Justice) is revealing. "James' father had quite a lot of the Scot somewhere in his ancestry, possibly a connection with the Robertsons?" claims Roderick Bromley, son of one of Justices' oldest and most cherished friends Toby Bromley. "James' father actively detested the Scots, considered that they infested the world, found them conceited and maudlin and scorned their humour, hated the bagpipes and mocked Burns Night. James, perhaps as a reaction to this, insisted that he was a true Scot who had first seen the light of day (underneath a distillery!) in Skye. I think that if you find a Robertson connection through the bloodline of James's father; you will have satisfactorily

The 1924-1925 Beckenham RUFC 1st XV – JRJ, aged just 17, is standing on the back row (3rd from left) along with Johnny Craddock (5th from left), future husband of TV Chef, Fanny. (Beckenham Rugby Club)

explained the almost pathological adoption of that country and customs by a paternally misunderstood boy from Kent"[2]

One can understand such a white lie about being born in Scotland, due to his family's roots, but why then did Justice also tell falsehoods about the year he was born, insisting it was 1905 when it was in fact 15 June 1907. Why did he wish to claim he was older than he actually was?

James was an only child, his father James Norval Justice, born in Aberdeen on 25 May 1876, was an eminent geologist and mining engineer whose work took him to such exotic places as Africa and Siam. James had a love/fear relationship with his father. His criticisms of the man were often rounded off by excusing him on the grounds that, as a mining engineer, he had spent much of his life in Africa in atrocious working conditions.[3]

James Norval Justice studied at Durham College of Science, confusingly then based in Newcastle upon Tyne, between 1893 and 1895, passing his exams with distinction and also making something of a name for himself on the university sports fields. He was described in the Durham University Journal of

23 March 1895 as: "right half. Quick and energetic. Plays well some days, but on others is entirely 'off.' Kicks wildly, but always tries."

Continuing his education at the Royal School of Mines in London, where he emerged as ARSM (Second Class – Mining) in 1898, Norval Justice then tried a spot of mineral prospecting in Northern Rhodesia (now Zambia) in what we would today call a gap year. Returning to Durham he took his BSc, passing with honours, in papers for Geology, for which he earned a distinction, Mineralogy and Crystallography. Between 1901 and 1906 he worked as surveyor, prospector and manager on West Africa's Gold Coast.

For a year he was based in Siam, Thailand today, but returned to the Gold Coast in 1907 to take charge of prospecting for the Ashanti Goldfield Corporation, where he discovered the mine that would eventually be named after him. During this hectic period, he found time to marry Edith Burgess, a nurse and 'frustrated' concert pianist and the couple had their one and only child, but fatherhood failed to impede on Justice's travels around the world. For much of the First World War he was prospecting for tin in northern Nigeria, but from 1917 to 1918, he was making explosives. Shortly after the end of the conflict, from 1919 to 1920, he was dredging for gold in Demerara and from 1920 to 1921 prospecting in Murmansk.

Unsurprisingly Norval Justice saw very little of his son growing up and when he returned home in 1922 the boy was already attending boarding school. Norval was back in England to estimate "gravels in the Thames valley" – hardly as romantic as gold prospecting, so one wonders if he had perhaps fallen on hard, post-war, times. It also perhaps explains why early in 1924, he fell in with William Paterson, later Forbes-Leslie, a crooked surgeon and geological con artist. Forbes-Leslie was behind a scam that had convinced many in Norfolk to hunt for oil in their Kimmeridge Clay. When that failed, rather expensively, he moved on to Somerset, where he purported to have discovered 'rich [Lias] oil shales' in the region. James Norval Justice provided an "amazing, expert," report on these shales in February 1924 and this helped Forbes-Leslie claim that these deposits in Somerset were the largest in volume and richest in yield, "of which the whole world's oil experts have knowledge." Forbes-Leslie set up a crooked operation to retrieve these shales, hoping to extract what was hardly there in the first place. One Grade 2 listed retort survives at Kilve, a wonderful monument to British lunacy in listening to such a crook. A marvellous character for sure, Forbes-Leslie, at the ripe old age of 70, would serve two years imprisonment for another case of fraud.

As for Norval Justice, he returned to prospecting in the Sudan in 1924 and continued to be active as a mineral prospector throughout Africa until early in

1945. He finally retired to Hillingbourne, near Maidstone, Kent, where he died on 29 March 1953.[4]

Little is known of James Robertson Justice's childhood, mainly because he seemed never to talk of it. Perhaps the absence of a father during long periods of his upbringing was too deep a wound to revisit. What is documented is his path through education. His first port of call was Marlborough College, Wiltshire, a top class public school founded in 1843, whose old boys include Anthony Blunt, John Betjeman, Siegfried Sassoon and the actors James Mason, Wilfrid Hyde-White and Ernest Thesiger. The college was built beside a mound; all that remains of a Norman castle. There are speculations that the Marlborough Mound is actually of much more ancient construction. One legend claims that it is where the great magician Merlin is imprisoned, having foolishly fallen in love in his old age with a pretty young girl.[5] One wonders how much of an effect such a myth had on the impressionable mind and imagination of the young Justice.

Upon arrival at Marlborough in the spring of 1921 Justice was assigned to one of the various houses where pupils lived and made their home while at school. His boarding house for the first couple of terms was Upcot and after that his senior house was Cotton, where his Housemaster was a Mr. A. H. Wall. The young Justice's education was solid, if unspectacular as his academic record below shows:

Summer 1921	Form: Shell	(Final position 68th out of 89)
Michaelmas 1921	Remove	(Final position 40th out of 104)
Lent 1922	Hundred	(Final position 51th out of 117)
Summer 1922	Hundred	(Final position 34th out of 127)
Michaelmas 1922	Science 5th	(12th out of 19)
Lent 1923	Science 5th	(8th out of 20)
Summer 1923	Science 5th	(12th out of 20)
Michaelmas 1923	Science L.VIth	(17th out of 20)
Lent 1924	Science L.VIth	(7th out of 19)
Summer 1924	Science L.VIth	(5th out of 17)

As is common in schools of this type the houses competed against one another in sports, and Justice played in goal for Cotton House at hockey and as a front row forward in their Rugby XV, both in his final year. Rugby was a sport that the already fearsome and bulky Justice excelled at. During the 1925-26 season he played in the first fifteen for Beckenham Rugby Club alongside Johnny Craddock, future husband of TV's first celebrity cook Fanny Craddock.

Justice left Marlborough College in the summer of 1924 to further his education at University College London, but only studied there for a single academic year, taking an intermediate Science course which included geology, physics, chemistry and zoology, with a dash of German thrown into the mix. Justice would make an unexpected return to UCL in 1954 for the film that would make his name: *Doctor in the House*. The magnificent front entrance of the college, designed by William Wilkins, who went on to build the National Gallery, was used as the exterior of the fictional medical school St Swithin's. In the film, Justice can clearly be seen striding across the front quad as the irascible surgeon Sir Lancelot Spratt. After he was famous Justice acknowledged his UCL roots when he returned as guest of honour at the dinner of the departmental student society, the Greenough Club, in the late 1960s.

A second language would prove useful when Justice enrolled in 1926 as a student of geology at Bonn University. Was this a serious attempt to follow in his father's footsteps? What is for sure is that one of his professors was the distinguished geologist and palaeontologist Gustav Steinmann. Justice, however, only lasted until the summer of 1927 and although his Times obituary (3 July 1975) ambiguously recorded how, "he went on to get his PhD at Bonn" there is no record of his graduation. Bonn University have since confirmed that he did not graduate

[1] Author interview with Roderick Bromley – 19th January 2007

[2] Author interview with Roderick Bromley – 19th January 2007

[3] Torrens, Hugh, *Justice Denied*, Geoscientist Magazine, April 2002

[4] Torrens, Hugh, *Justice Denied*, Geoscientist Magazine, April 2002

[5] Chandler, John *'Marlborough and Eastern Wiltshire'* – Hobnob Press (2001)

CHAPTER 2:
VANCOUVER VIA FLEET STREET

Justice once claimed that during his lifetime he must have had around seventy jobs, but after leaving Bonn and dispensing with geology altogether on his return to London, it appears that his first choice of career was journalism. In 1929, he was a reporter for the news agency Reuters, when it was still based in Carmelite Street, just off Fleet Street, home then to the British newspaper industry. One of Reuters' more competent reporters, A.D. Skene, claimed that "the average recruit appears to have no intention of becoming a journalist." He went on to mention two examples: "Messrs Jesse and Justice – excellent fellows, no doubt, but quite unsuitable."[1] This was at a time when a journalist's background was considered more important than his aptitude for shorthand.

Justice's time with Reuters may have been short-lived but it was far from uneventful, coinciding as it did with that of Ian Fleming, creator of James Bond. Already Justice's playful nature was rising to the surface, for when he worked on the nightshift he would present himself in dressing gown and pyjamas. Such eccentricity no doubt endeared him to his superiors as he managed to avoid being sacked on at least one occasion. Reuters was ruled by the autocratic Sir Roderick Jones who one day was sat in the back seat of his car outside the office when he was surprised to find a sheet of Reuters' copy plummeting from an open window, in the guise of a paper plane. When the offending object had landed, an uneasy silence fell over the entire office. The staff waited for the call from Sir Roderick and eventually the telephone rang and Justice was summoned forth. A few minutes later and Justice appeared, apparently none the worse for wear and still employed.[2] When he finally did leave the news desk at Reuters, his replacement was a certain Douglas Slocombe,[3] later a noted cinematographer who made his name with Ealing films and went on to photograph the Indiana Jones movies and many other classics.

In spite of his foray into journalism Justice's father had always dreamed that his son would win a position with the Foreign Office. Predictably Justice took extreme measures to avoid such a fate – by emigrating to Canada. And so on 1 November 1929, Justice was on board the Duchess of Richmond, as she sailed for Quebec, giving his occupation as journalist, his nationality as British but his race of people as Scottish. As he was still only 22, his father paid for his passage.[4]

The voyage to Canada took an immense seven days and Justice arrived, exhausted no doubt, but excited at the world of new possibilities that might open up for him. He was in for a rude awakening. After one or two days in Quebec he made the four-day journey by train over to Vancouver, British Columbia. Justice hoped that the experience gained working at Reuters, which was after all one of Europe's most celebrated news agencies, might put him in good stead for a similar position in Vancouver. Alas, by the time of his arrival the great depression had struck and unemployment was rife. He applied for a job at the Vancouver Sun newspaper but the answer was a swift, "sorry, no." Ironically 21 years later, whilst staying with Dilys' (Justice's first wife) sister and her family in Vancouver during a film promotion tour of Canada, Justice dropped in at the newsroom of the Sun reflecting with good humour about his earlier rejection.[5]

For the next two months, Justice toiled at insurance but didn't sell, "a single blessed policy." After a few weeks he won a job as an English master at Shawnigan Lake Boy's School, situated forty-five minutes north of Victoria on the shores of Shawnigan Lake. It was a well respected but typical prep school and corporal punishment was often used, except in Justice's case. Rather than resort to physical violence when one of his young charges misbehaved, Justice merely employed the power of his already volcanic voice, to subdue any errant pupil. This was enough to reduce any miscreant into a puddle on the floor and was considered a much more effective admonishment. There is no record that Justice ever taught again, but it was clear, as a committed socialist that he was aware how important education was to young people. But Justice didn't hold down this position for long. As he later confessed to a relative, "I got fired – and deservedly so." He liked to maintain that he lost the post because he flung a piece of chalk at a pupil and hit him on the nose. No doubt that particular pupil could not be subdued by Justice's roars alone.

A succession of jobs followed, he drove a truck in Oregon and mined for gold. His good friend Sir Peter Scott recalled that Justice once told him that he even served a spell in the Canadian Mounties. Almost certainly fabrication as becoming a member of the Royal Canadian Mounted Police was (and still is) an extremely long and arduous process. One other profession that Justice certainly *did* try his hand at was laying carpets, including those in Victoria's most prestigious hotel, The Empress. After a trip to Canada in 1958 promoting the Ralph Thomas film, *Campbell's Kingdom*, Justice wrote to Dilys' sister and her husband, Olwyn & James Thomson, about what it had felt like returning to the country for the first time since 1929: "It was fun being in Vancouver again, especially under the rather changed circumstances compared to my first visit. I only wish I could have gone to The Empress in Victoria, to see whether the carpets I laid are still there."[6] The Empress still stands (with new carpets) and is now known as The Fairmont Express

[1]   Reuters Archive

[2]   Reuters Archive

[3]   Ettedgui, Peter *'Cinematography'* – Focal Press (2001) p17

[4]   National Archives of Canada

[5]   The Vancouver Sun – Tuesday 20th February 1951, p 12

[6]   Letter written 14th April 1958. Courtesy of Jamie Thomson

Whitney Straight (seated) and JRJ (right) setting off to practice for the International Trophy at Brooklands in 1933

CHAPTER 3:
JUSTICE ON ICE

By 1931 Justice had returned home; his Canadian odyssey ending rather ignominiously, with him working his passage back to Blighty as a dishwasher on a Dutch freighter. Back in London he threw himself into the sporting world, notably ice hockey, not a sport one would have readily associated with Justice, given his not inconsiderable size, even then. Perhaps his time in Canada had given him a rudimentary knowledge of the game, as the sport was much more advanced in that country than in Europe. His enthusiasm and familiarity with the game must have ensured he was a skilled exponent on the ice, since he played in goal during the 1931/32 season for the London Lions,[1] when their home stadium was at the Golders Green Ice Rink, North London. Indeed, a net minder requires incredible agility and skill.

Forced to retire from the game after a skiing injury, Justice became assistant secretary of the British Ice Hockey Association for a year and also managed to keep a hand in the physical side of the sport with the odd bit of refereeing. The most eventful match at which he officiated took place at Golders Green Ice Rink in the spring of 1932. It involved the England team and Vienna EV, who represented Austria. When the Austrian net minder was sent to the penalty box for an infringement, the rest of the team took umbrage and vacated the ice. It took the intervention of the Austrian ambassador to persuade his countrymen to return to the ice and resume the game to avoid an international incident!

Justice also managed Great Britain at the European Championships held in Berlin from 14 to 20 March of the same year. Team GB finished a respectable seventh.[2]

Justice then left the world of ice hockey, though still harboured an interest in the sport as a spectator. During the late fifties and early sixties, he could often be seen in attendance at the home matches of his local team, the Southampton Vikings, when he lived in Stockbridge, Hampshire. Indeed despite his considerable bulk later in life Justice remained remarkably fit, with a strong constitution. One of his friends, Martin Leslie, recalls an evening in the 1950s that demonstrates the point perfectly. The pair were at a party when an argument developed. "James, who'd had a few (we'd all had a few), was saying that the youth today were completely spineless, they're no good for anything. They're not fit for a start. "In my day." etc, etc. I was, luckily, at that time frighteningly fit because I was part of an athletic team and so I said: 'Come-on James, I'll take you on, climb up any hill, and go anywhere.' 'No, no, no,' he said. 'I can't do that, but swimming. I can certainly do the swimming.' So I challenged him to a 2 lengths race in the Inverness swimming bath.

"The details of the bet were being sorted out (there would be a purse on the side of about five guineas) and people in the party were agreeing to be witnesses, when a chap called Geordie Dudgeon appeared on the scene and said: 'Why wait? Why don't we go and do it now?' It was 11 o'clock at night. 'I've got a duck pond, not very far away. Why don't we have the competition there? Two lengths, across and back.' So James said, 'Certainly...lead-on!'" The group arrived at this 'pond' which was in fact a small dam mill pond, about 30 yards wide and a Land Rover was parked as close by as it could get to light the surface of the water. Both Justice and Leslie were given a second of a beautiful young woman and stepped to the water's edge. They had already stripped except for their kilts and when the starting shot went-off, courtesy of a 12 bore shotgun, both men ripped the kilt off, handed it to the second and dived-in. "I remember it being absolutely, frighteningly, bitterly cold," says Leslie. "And I also remember that I couldn't beat James across. He was in front of me and I could make absolutely no impression on him. I was swallowing his kick. So I was about a body's length behind him when we reached the shore on the other side. We can't have gone more than 20 yards when we grounded. Now, he beached himself, like a whale, and roaring with laughter, he tried to get himself turned-round. I got turned-round much faster and got back to the other side, beating him hands down. An awful silence followed because we couldn't hear him swimming. We couldn't see him swimming and there wasn't a sound from him."

Everyone got worried. Geordie Dudgeon and the other people said, "My God, what's happened to him?" They looked across at Leslie and implored him to get back in and get across and see what on earth was going on. "So, absolutely crucifyingly cold as the water was I had to get back into it, and swim across to the other side. No sign of him at all, anywhere." Leslie got back out, extremely worried. "I can't find him – maybe he's sunk!" Everyone looked stunned at each other and someone was quickly sent to bring more lights. Then, all of a sudden, they heard this dreadful, throaty laugh from the dam and the thump of a leg kicking in the water, followed by a spout of spray rising up to hit the headlights of the land rover. Again, there was this roar of laughter. "He was over by the sluice gate," recalls Leslie. "Hanging onto it, completely impervious to the cold, well-padded as he was, laughing himself sick that we'd actually thought he'd drowned! Anyway, I was deputed to go and get him, just in case he couldn't make it on his own, which of course he could."

Finally Justice arrived at the side of the bank and demanded that everybody pull him out. Then at the crucial moment he put his full weight upon those poor men and women trying to get him out, hoping to pull them back into the water with him. But they let go and because Justice's grip was wet he fell back in with a monumental plonk! "He was laughing so hard," says Leslie. "People were very nervous about being pulled-in and I was eventually persuaded to go in again and get him out as I was the only one who was wet. "Get your shoulder under his bum and push him out." They suggested. Well I got my shoulder under his bum, he thought that was the funniest thing on this earth, and as soon as he sat on me we disappeared with a huge splash and soaked most of the spectators. I was lucky to have survived the whole thing, but anyway, eventually, with me pushing and people pulling we got him out. It was an experience I shall never forget. I was so cold that my teeth were chattering. He wasn't bothered at all. The hot baths and large drams we got were VERY much appreciated."[3]

After trying out rugby at school, then ice hockey, the next sport to catch Justice's interest was motor racing. At Brooklands, on 16th May 1932, Justice entered his Frazer Nash for Le Mans veteran, Roy Eccles, although it is not clear which one of them drove it. Justice also partnered a H.H.Wanborough driving a Wolseley Hornet in the Junior Car Club 1000 mile race at Brooklands, on the 3rd and 4th of June, 1932[4] They retired after completing 397 miles and the race was eventually won by the celebrated female drivers, Elsie Wisdom and Joan Richmond, the first women ever to win a major international motor race against male competitors.[5]

By 1933 he'd retired from competitive racing (but not before qualifying to become a member of the British Racing Drivers Club) and became involved in the Whitney Straight driving team. Straight was quite a character and one can imagine Justice getting on rather well with him. Born in New York, Straight moved to England when his American heiress mother remarried, and began racing while still an undergraduate at Cambridge, competing all around Europe. Straight raced in more Grand Prix than any American until after World War II. In 1933 driving a Maserati he won the Donington Trophy and the Mountain Championship, and in 1934 formed his own motor racing team, aged still only twenty-one, personally driving to victory in the South African Grand Prix.[6]

But flying was Straight's real passion. At the age of 16 years, too young for a pilot's licence, Straight had already achieved over 60 hours solo flight. During World War II, he flew Hurricanes in the Battle of Britain, was shot down over France in August of 1941 but managed to escape a German POW camp. At the war's end he became chairman of the Royal Aero Club and while still in his thirties deputy chairman of British Overseas Airways Corporation (BOAC), later British Airways. He was also deputy chairman of Rolls-Royce. Flight must have run in the family's blood as in the United States, his cousin Cornelius Vanderbilt Whitney was the President of Aviation Corporation of America which ultimately became Pan American Airways.[7]

Far from an amateur outfit for enthusiasts, the Whitney Straight racing team was from the outset a highly professional business venture that not only included Straight's brother Michael and his own chauffeur but numerous friends, including Justice. One of several people who hung around the periphery of the team, Justice became a factotum of sorts for Straight. One of his first jobs was to travel to the Maserati factory in Bologna to pick up their latest model, Maserati 8CM number 3011, as it had the new specifications for the forthcoming Grand Prix Season of 1934.[8]

Then Justice's life was to take an unexpected turn.

[1] A to Z Encyclopaedia of Ice Hockey (www.azhockey.com)

[2] British Ice Hockey Association (now Ice Hockey UK) archive

[3] Author interview with Martin Leslie – Isle of Skye – 2007

[4] Brooklands Museum Archive

[5] www.historicracing.com

[6] Obituary – The Times 10 April, 1979

[7] Obituary – The Times 10 April, 1979

[8] www.historicracing.com – drivers section

CHAPTER 4:
FIGHTING MAN

From ice hockey and motor cars, Justice suddenly found himself in military uniform and second in command of the League of Nations Police Force in Saar between 1934 and 1935. The Saar was an area of Germany that bordered with France and which after the First World War was put under League of Nations control. In 1933, a considerable number of anti-Nazi Germans fled to the Saar, as it was the only remaining part of Germany that was not under the political control of the Third Reich. Skirmishes were not uncommon, but Justice caused an international incident when he shot a Nazi Party member in the leg and was duly reprimanded with a court martial. This incident might even have been more serious according to one of Justice's friends Jonathan Dalrymple-Smith: "I can't guarantee the truth of this, but I heard from a separate source that James, while serving with the Army of Occupation in the Saar, drew a pistol when surrounded by a hostile crowd, fired at the ground and killed a civilian with the ricochet. However, I emphasise that I don't know the truth of that."[1]

Betty Box, who produced several of Justice's films, once recalled glancing at a newspaper clipping of the incident, and also had a strong feeling that Justice had been involved with Military Intelligence at the time, as his knowledge of languages would have been of great use.[1] Betty herself took full advantage of Justice's linguistic skills when they were both in Athens for the shooting of *Doctor at Sea* in 1955. The production company organised a soiree for several of the embassies and Justice was the life and soul of the party. He was able to talk and translate for all the different nationalities.[2]

Justice never spoke much about his time in the League of Nations Police Force but it obviously meant quite a lot to him since he hung a photograph of himself in uniform in the living room of his most beloved of homes in Spinningdale. One day Roderick Bromley, the young son of family friend Toby Bromley, saw it and asked Justice about it and was told that he had been a member of the international force which made up the Ruhr police, specifically guarding the railways, prior to the annexation by Hitler of that part of Germany. And here Roderick reveals another incident involving Justice: "Apparently he and a friend of his beat up a Nazi sympathiser, Jew baiter or whatever, either to the point of death or, depending on your romantic streak, past that point. He then had to leave the Ruhr in a big hurry because the Germans, quite rightly, regarded his GBH/murder offence in a rather serious light. I actually do not know if he ever went back to Germany after the war. I suppose that if he did, any police record would have lost its criminality and been placed instead on the folk hero shelf."[3]

Obviously getting a taste for action, Justice then fought in 1936 with the International Brigade against General Franco's fascists during the Spanish Civil War. The International Brigade was a volunteer army consisting of artists, intellectuals and workers who were committed to the republican cause. One volunteer, an Irishman by the name of Joe Monks, wrote of his time with the anti-fascists in his 1985 book 'With the Reds in Andalusia.' In it he recalled being allocated to an English-speakers' company in Madrigueras, where he was ordered to report to a certain Captain James Justice. Monks and his comrades were on their uppers and needed fresh boots. "Justice was obliged to open up the store room and allowed us to pick out left and right boots which were suitable for size from a collection of footwear that had been thrown together into a heap," Monks wrote. "Our difficulties in finding boots to match gave him a chance to indulge in a dash of what was to be, in a future career, his stock in trade – irascibility."[4]

After that minor encounter Justice was no more. "Within a day or two he had disappeared from our midst and we never again saw or heard of him in Spain," wrote Monks. The reason for Justice's rather hasty departure from the country (apart from a badly injured knee) may have had something to do with the fact that there was a price on his head. After the war, Justice befriended the naturalist and artist Keith Shackleton who recalled, "James had been in Spain fighting the fascists, where, incidentally, he acquired a price on his head. I'm afraid I forget what the price was but I know that it was a considerable sum of money."[5]

Within a few years General Franco and his regime would prove victorious in Spain, but Justice would see action again in the Second World War with the Royal Navy Volunteer Reserve (RNVR). It's believed that sometime either late in 1940 or early 1941 Justice enlisted with the RNVR and was placed with their engineering branch,[5] despite a total ignorance of anything to do with engines. The RNVR would play a crucial part in Britain's armed forces during the war. Referred to as the 'Wavy Navy' after the wavy gold braid officers wore on their sleeves, the RNVR were recruits accepted by the Royal Navy for the duration of hostilities, becoming temporary officers and serving only until the fighting ceased when they would be demobilised. Besides Justice other notable 'celebrity' volunteers were Laurence Olivier and Ralph Richardson.

By February 1941, Justice had been promoted to Sub-Lieutenant (E), E being for Engineering, and was known to have served on two ships. Firstly the MV Georgic, launched in 1931, the last passenger liner built in Cunard's fateful series of ships that included the Titanic. In 1940 it was converted by the Ministry of War into a troop ship for 3,000 men. In July 1941, the Georgic arrived at Port Tewfik in the Gulf of Suez, part of a convoy which had to be left almost unprotected during the hunt for the German warship Bismarck. She arrived safely on 7th July 1941, but a week later on 14th July she was bombed by German aircraft while at anchor off Port Tewfik, with 800 Italian internees on board. Her fuel oil caught fire and the ammunition exploded in the stern area. The gutted out ship was beached on a reef to prevent her from sinking and later the decision was made to salvage the vessel and undergo extensive repairs. The work took several months so without a ship Justice was sent aboard HMS Edinburgh Castle, then stationed in the hot, sticky environs of Freetown, the capital of Sierra Leone, where it was used for naval personnel and survivors of sunken ships. After the war HMS Edinburgh Castle was deemed not cost effective to tow back to England and so it was sunk by gunfire and depth charges.

Justice survived his time at sea but ceased active service with RNVR in 1943. A profile of the actor in a 1952 Picture Post magazine[6] refers to an injury sustained by a German shell as having ended his wartime service with the Navy. On being sent ashore Justice was ordered up to Lossiemouth in Scotland, situated on the Moray Firth, to work on the runways for the local Royal Naval Air Station. Whilst in Lossiemouth, Justice met Captain James Brander Dunbar, better known as The Laird of Pitgaveny. The two men had a great deal in common and got on extremely well, with The Laird often inviting Justice up Pitgaveny to shoot. Martin Leslie also made The Laird's acquaintance as a young boy, long before he met Justice. "From the age of 16 until I went in to National Service I spent a lot of time up at Pitgaveny. And I often went back to see The

Laird until he died – aged 93. I remember he claimed to be the last man alive to have been shot at in anger by bow and arrow. This was during the second Matabele War, just before the Boer War!"

For the remainder of World War Two and a few years after that, Justice was based in idyllic circumstances in and around the small town of Wigtown in south west Scotland. Now boasting the largest local nature reserve in Britain, when Justice was living there he spent much of his time shooting the local goose population. This is most likely the reason why he settled in the area, having been informed by his close friend Peter Scott of the opportunities for shooting game. Justice appeared to make his living in the district as a wildfowler, shooting geese and selling the birds, and for decades after was well remembered by several locals as a colourful character in what was a rather staid rural town. One local referred to Justice as "Whiskers" – the beard, famous even then, was often matted with mud from the 'inks', as the foreshore of Wigtown Bay was called. Another, Roy McKie, remembered how Justice supplied his father with plastic tubs of Navy stores tobacco on a regular basis.[7] Even though Justice was no longer a serving officer, he did become an honourary member of the nearby RAF training ground Officers' Mess, spending a great deal of time there. He was also a frequent visitor to the Grapes Inn pub, where he associated with all and sundry, local folk or farmers with money. His Rolls Royce made him the talk of the town and when asked how he squared his car with his left-wing politics, he merely replied that when the revolution came he would simply convert it into an armoured vehicle.

When he first arrived in Wigtown, many wondered why since he was clearly of conscription age and apparently in rude health, was he not serving in the forces? Rumours at the time suggested that he was an intelligence officer who "knew too much" and had been sent to this remote part of Britain to lessen the likelihood of him being captured by the Germans. He was an exceptional linguist, being fluent in numerous European languages including various Balkan dialects. It is said that Justice had various friends in the Intelligence Service, including Ian Fleming. This theory is backed up by the fact that Justice was a regular guest at the Officers' Mess at nearby Baldoon Aerodrome. He was also known to have stayed in Troon under the name of "Lieutenant Robertson" at the time the Ayrshire town was the base for Lord Lovat's No. 4 Commando Squadron.

According to friend Roger Upton, Justice did indeed indulge in a bit of James Bond-type espionage after he came out of the navy. "Rumour had it that at that time he worked for MI5 (or British Intelligence) and was sent over to Germany on some sort of mission. If you think about it, he was perfect for this kind of work as he spoke the language fluently and had spent time there. Well, apparently he was sent over there to meet a chap and collect something that must have been very important. God only knows what it was, but after arriving at the rendezvous point he was promptly tapped on the shoulder by a chap who handed him the said envelope and was promptly shot dead. But not before he told James to get it to MI5 as soon as he could. James naturally scarpered before he was too was shot and duly escaped back to London. God knows how!"

When he first arrived in Wigtown, Justice was a paying guest at a boarding house, along with Keith 'Toby' Bromley, destined to be a long serving friend. They met in the Royal Navy Volunteer Reserve, where Bromley was supervising the supply of tank landing-craft. Toby had begun his career in the family shoe business, Russell & Bromley, and later became a noted benefactor to the causes of conservation and human rights. Good-looking and blessed with endless energy, Bromley might have followed a conventional career but for a deep fund of sensitivity inadequately disguised by a brusque manner. Later, having helped to transform Russell & Bromley from a local shoe company into a leader in fashion, he created the Wyld Court Rainforest, a corner of Amazonia set in Berkshire, and an inspiration for Cornwall's universally acclaimed Eden Project.

The two men had grown close because of their joint love for wildfowling. The Lincolnshire prize-fighter and wildfowler Kenzie Thorpe wrote in admiration of Bromley: "Toby was a real hard case. Every hair on his head was a rope yarn. Every spot of blood Stockholm tar. He didn't feel the cold, nor frost, nor nothing. Nothing put him off his wildfowling and he turned out to be a very good wildfowler indeed and a very good shot."[8] Bromley would later use his experience to establish an internationally famous collection of rare geese and ducks at his home in Hampshire.

Now in her seventies, Sarah Trew was a little girl of 11 when Justice arrived in Wigtown to stay at her mother's house, but still remembers him clearly. "He stayed with us for about a year with his friend, Toby Bromley. I remember it being said that there was a price on his head when he stayed with my mother. On New Year's Day he was out shooting geese. During the shoot he injured a goose and actually swam across the river Cree to put it out of its misery. It was an extremely cold day and the Cree was part covered in thin ice[9]

Justice moved around the town after that, staying for a while with a Nellie McDowall. Her cousin remembers that after breakfast, Justice would leave to shoot at the local ducks, doing the same thing after the evening meal. The garage was where he used to hang the dead geese and ducks, gossips suggesting that his methods of shooting being not entirely legal. Miss McDowall's cousin, in hindsight, was surprised that Justice had been a lodger at all, as his landlady was a rather prim lady who was very against blood sports![10]

Eventually Justice settled in a large house on Agnew Crescent. "Orchaton was its name," recalls Susan Trew. "And he pulled out the fireplace in the lounge and just left a hole in the wall. He also painted the walls with wildlife scenes."[11] This is where Justice set up home, having met and married Dilys Ethel Hayden, the ceremony taking place on 13th February 1941 at Chelsea Register Office situated on The Kings Road. Dilys was a trainee nurse and the couple had lived with her parents in Epping for a short while prior to the wedding. Dilys' father was a coal merchant. Justice's occupation at the time, according to the marriage certificate, was Civil Engineer. He'd set up a company clearing bomb damage using bulldozers. He also used his bulldozer for road work, including laying the foundations for the A1.

After his few years of flamboyant, if impecunious, living in Wigtown, Justice pulled off an extraordinary 'midnight flit', selling his house and moving south leaving a long list of unpaid debts. The many individuals and establishments that were never paid included the late Nellie McDowall, guesthouse owner in Bladnoch, and the late Gordon Henry, the Wigtown petrol stockist.

Justice clearly enjoyed his time living in the town, spending many carefree days wildfowling in Wigtown Bay, fishing for salmon on the Bladnoch, Cree and Luce, and providing lively company at any drinks party going. Several sources and reference books have actually given his place of birth as Wigtown, an erroneous fact no doubt begun by Justice himself. But the most remarkable thing must surely be the affection with which Justice is remembered by the populace of Wigtown, despite his frequent reprehensible behaviour. The impecunious socialist being guest of honour at Wigtownshire society parties; the conservationist breaking the world record for shooting duck with a punt gun; the expert fly fisherman using dynamite in the best salmon pools of the Cree; the fighting-fit civilian dining in the Officers' Mess at Baldoon; the successful actor reneging on his bills. The list of contradictions seems never-ending, yet Justice remains still a popular figure in Wigtown, the place he adopted as his home. So much so that on 25th September 2005, Wigtown Book Festival hosted a unique tribute to the late, great man. Tickets were £8, but anyone producing an original unsettled account in the name of James Robertson Justice was admitted for free!![12]

[1] Correspondence with author, 24th January 2007
[2] Author interview with Betty Box at Pinewood Studios – 1994
[3] Box, Betty E.'Lifting The Lid' – The Book Guild (2000), p 111
[4] www.unithistories.com
[5] www.greatoceanliners.net

[6] Picture Post, February 21st 1953

[7] Author interview, September 2005

[8] Obituary, Daily Telegraph, 29th August 2003

[9] Letter to Author – 2004

[10] Ibid

[11] Ibid

[12] http://www.wigtownbookfestival.com/

CHAPTER 5:
AN ACTOR'S LIFE BECKONS

Justice always liked to say that he fell into acting by extraordinary chance, as it was a profession he'd never given a single thought about following. It started at the beginning of 1943 at 10 Albemarle Street, London, then the home of the world-famous Players Theatre Club, of which Justice was a member and frequent visitor.

The history of The Players Theatre is a microcosm of British theatrical history, and many famous names have appeared on its stage. At its conception in 1936, the Players was intended as a club, covering many aspects of theatrical entertainment. The founders, Leonard Sachs and Peter Ridgeway, acquired premises on the top floor of 43 Kings Street, Covent Garden, and rapidly established the Players' reputation, with Victorian music hall turns proving the most popular.[1]

When Ridgeway died of TB, at the age of just 34, Sachs continued on his own, his gift for discovering new talent being a major factor in his success. Among the new recruits came Bernard Miles and Peter Ustinov (auditioning at 11 am, onstage by 11 pm) in what was his professional debut. Soon The Players Theatre was recognised by public and critics as, 'the most original entertainment in London.' It was even endorsed as one of the clubs to which the subalterns of the Household Brigade were permitted to belong. The Churchill family were great supporters too, Sarah Churchill helping as a programme seller. Sir Maurice and Lady Violet Bonham-Carter, together with their son, Mark, are to be found amongst the early membership, which included many leading members of London society.

The outbreak of the Second World War in 1939 inevitably caused serious problems. The Players' premises, on the top floor of an old building with a glass roof and a hydraulic lift, were not an ideal venue during an air-raid. Eventually, the theatre found a refuge at 10 Albemarle Street in the former El Morocco Night Club. This was in a basement in one of the few concrete buildings in London. Thanks to this good fortune, the Players' (along with The Windmill) never closed throughout the War.[2]

Leonard Sachs was called up for military service and turned over the running of his beloved theatre to Jean Anderson, already an established actress and Players' artiste. Under her management, the Players' became a haven for Londoners suffering the Blitz, as well as a home from home for many of the Allied forces also living in London. Americans, Australians, Canadians, Czechs, Danes, Dutch, the Free French, Indians, New Zealanders, Norwegians, Poles, Rhodesians, and South Africans – all were to be found among the Players' audience.[3]

One particular evening Justice was serving in the vanguard of the audience in the banter that is exchanged with the compere, when his obvious boisterous nature struck the management as being ideal chairman material, someone to introduce the various acts. The regular chairman was ill and so Justice was asked to fill-in for a few weeks. He leapt at the chance. Always a fine speaker and raconteur, the owners of the club were convinced they'd asked the right chap to step in, and they were right, Justice was an instant hit in the role. No real acting was required, he could just be himself, and while delivering this impromptu performance he was spotted by Ealing writer/director Harry Watt and rewarded with his first film appearance, as an Operations Room Officer in *For Those in Peril* (1944), for which Watt was co-scripting.

Justice's name failed to make the credits but it would establish a long association with the famous Ealing Studios in the post-war era, and the money was useful, too, paying for flies for fishing and cartridges for shooting. The film's director was a newcomer too, making his debut behind the camera was Charles Crichton who would go on to direct the Ealing classics *The Lavender Hill Mob* and *The Titfield Thunderbolt*, as well as the 80s comedy hit *A Fish Called Wanda*.

Next Harry Watt cast Justice in *Fiddlers Three* (1944), a comedy vehicle he was directing for the popular cockney stand-up comic Tommy Trinder. The plot, such as it was, had Trinder and a couple of pals travelling back in time to ancient Rome. Cast as a centurion, Justice's first credited role, the film wasn't a huge success yet it made him realise that he might be able to make a lot of money out of something he found quite easy.

As for the Players Theatre, which inadvertently had helped launch Justice's career in movies, the venue went from strength to strength after the war. Leonard Sachs returned to take up the reins again and was immediately obliged to seek yet another location, ending up at Villiers Street in premises under Charing Cross Station, the site of a former theatre. The Club continued to discover new talent; Hattie Jacques, Bill Owen, Ian Carmichael and Clive Dunn appeared regularly on the bill, along with Patsy Rowlands and Maggie Smith.

The Players' Theatre Club was certainly unique in its quest to keep alive the traditions and songs of Victorian music hall and survived unfunded and unsponsored until 2002 when it was forced to close its doors. But tradition isn't so easily buried, and in recent years the Club has risen again, performing around ten shows a year in a theatre called The Venue, just off Leicester Square in the heart of London's West End.[4]

[1]   The Players Theatre archive (www.playerstheatre.co.uk)

[2]   Ibid

[3]   Ibid

[4]   Ibid

CHAPTER 6:
THE WILDFOWLER

During the Spanish Civil War Justice was said to have brought one particular battle charge to a halt, when he pointed to the sky and cried: "Look! Greylag geese!"[1] Justice's lifelong love of wildfowling is just as much an important part of this fascinating man's story as his celebrated movies.

Justice was a founding member of the Severn Wildfowl Trust, established in November 1946 by one of his best friends, Peter Scott, son of the famous explorer Sir Robert Falcon Scott. Other founding members included wildlife artist Keith Shackleton and Field-Marshal Viscount Lord Allanbrooke. The Trust is now better known as the Wildfowl and Wetlands Trust and is located in Slimbridge, between Bristol & Gloucester.

Justice had been a friend of Peter Scott's from his punt gunning days. To the uninitiated, punt gunning is the use of a large bore shotgun, firing a charge of between eight and twenty ounces of shot, mounted cannon-like in the bow of a punt. Lying flat so as to give the smallest silhouette, the crew use hand paddles to stalk ducks on open water. If a shot can be achieved a number of ducks can be downed but it is extremely difficult. Few sports, wrote Elspeth Huxley in her biography of Sir Peter Scott, call for greater skill, endurance and self-discipline.[2]

Justice's own punt gun, Irish Tom, is an awesome piece of shooting history. Measuring over 14ft in length, it weighs 300lbs and is known to have once fired a thundering 3 lbs of shot!

JRJ & Prince Phillip on their one and only Punt Gunning expedition to The Wash in the early 1950's – joined by Toby Bromley (with JRJ) and Geoffrey Ivan Jones. (Roderick Bromley)

Acquired after the Second World War, Justice used Irish Tom on many of his trips on the Wash, including one with the Duke of Edinburgh in the early 1950's. The Wash, a shallow inlet of the North Sea on the east coast of England, between Lincolnshire and Norfolk is one of the few places that active punt gunning still takes place and it can be a perilous pastime. Two officers from the Argyll and Sutherland Highlanders were punt gunning on the river Alde in December 1932, when the charge detonated before the breech was properly shut. Fortunately an RAF officer, also wildfowling nearby, came to their assistance. Despite receiving emergency medical aid, neither the trained nurse on the scene or later the surgeon could avoid one man losing his leg and the other a hand.[3]

For a number of years Irish Tom was lost and is believed to have had a brief incarnation as a builder's scaffolding pole. Now of too large a bore to shoot waterfowl legally, it was rediscovered in an Inverness boatyard in 1981 and restored before being presented to BASC, where it sits today, on permanent display at their headquarters in Rossett.[4]So close was the friendship between Justice and Peter Scott that to this day a portrait of the actor hangs in the home of Sir Peter's widow Lady Philippa Scott. Scott was only too happy to bring Justice on board at the Trust and the men would set aside most weekends to focus on their joint endeavour. Justice came over from his home in Hampshire, usually with a case of Founder's Port (Sanderson 1917), while Peter Scott would drive at speed in his green Jaguar to review progress and re-energise everyone in sight. A sense of fun pervaded these gatherings of middle-aged adults all working for the same goal.[5]

During the summer of 1947, everyone got down to work hammering-in stakes, digging-out ponds, planting willows and, when the winter came, shivering in pill-boxes counting geese. One semi-tame bird of prey that lived at the centre and who was standoffish towards strangers, took a particular liking to Justice, allowing him to hold her while she nibbled his beard.[6]

In a television interview in the 60s Justice spoke about the Trust and its valuable place in the country's nature: "One of the sad things about the prosperity of this country is the fact that there are fewer and fewer Wetlands and of course Wetlands are places where waterfowl of the world can take sanctuary. These sanctuaries are becoming fewer and fewer and I'm afraid waterfowl are dying out. The Wildfowl Trust was started in order to protect and care for wildfowl on a more organised scale than had hitherto been done. We have had one considerable success with the Hawaiian Geese. They were down to less than forty in the world and thanks to an initiative undertaken by Peter Scott and his team there are now around three hundred. We have even been able to send some back to the Hawaiian Islands."[7]

Besides the Trust, Peter Scott invited Justice to help him out in a curious invention that is still in use today. To study wildfowl scientifically had, from the start, been one of Scott's major aims. The British Trust for Ornithology and the International Council for Bird Preservation had, for some years, been running a system of ringing birds, recovering the rings of those killed or dead from accidental or natural causes, and with this information mapping the migration routes of various species; but wild geese, being large and wary, were particularly difficult to catch, and methods of doing so were unsatisfactory. Before the War, Scott had experimented with possible solutions to the problem. Even when in the midst of planning the Allied invasion of France, his mind had reverted to the matter of netting wild geese and he believed he'd come up with a new way of catching them with a net propelled by rockets! It sounded truly outlandish but Scott was convinced it was practical. The idea came from a device to save the lives of drowning men: a lifebuoy was propelled by a rocket to come to rest within reach of the man in the sea. Scott invited Justice to come along with him to the factory that manufactured the device and set them the task of adapting it to propel a net instead of a lifebuoy. In February 1948 a trial of this adapted device took place and proved a success. The device that was the brainchild of Scott, and which Justice had a small but significant hand in, is still in use decades later.[8]

[1] Huxley, Elspeth *'Peter Scott: Painter & Naturalist'* (Faber & Faber 1995)

[2] Ibid

[3] Email to author from Graham Downing at The Shooting Times

[4] Author interview with Keith Shackleton – 2005

[5] Huxley, Elspeth *'Peter Scott: Painter & Naturalist'* (Faber & Faber 1995)

[6] Ibid

[7] Interview with Joan Bakewell – BBC Television – 1966 – last shown in 2004 as part of BBC4's 1960's season.

[8] Huxley, Elspeth *'Peter Scott: Painter & Naturalist'* (Faber & Faber 1995)

CHAPTER 7:
JUSTICE FOR USTINOV?

After minor appearances in a couple of forgettable British movies Justice landed the role that would change his film career forever, providing him with the template for the on-screen persona that he would exploit for the rest of his life. *Vice Versa* (1948) was based on F. Anstey's classic children's story of a boy and his father who exchange bodies with comic consequences. The plot is familiar today since it has been remade several times, notably as a vehicle for a young Jodie Foster in 1976's *Freaky Friday*, then again in 1987 for *Like Father Like Son* starring Dudley Moore, and again with Judge Reinhold in 1988.

Anstey's Victorian novel was adapted by Peter Ustinov, then only 26. Ustinov, the son of a Russian émigré, had been touted as Britain's answer to Orson Welles, having sold a screenplay in his early twenties and embarked on a career as a film director. *Vice Versa* was his second feature and he cast Justice largely because "he had fought in the Spanish Civil War on the side of unpopular legitimacy and been a collaborator of my father's in the early days at the Reuter's building in Blackfriars."[1]

Their first meeting did not bode well, as the two men spent nearly twenty minutes screaming at each other in German about nothing in particular, but they would remain good friends, sometimes one actually being mistaken for each other, especially during the 1950's when Ustinov sported a bushy beard. One day in Rome in the bar of the Excelsior Hotel on the Via Veneto, "which was always slightly Fellini-ish," recalled Ustinov, an extremely beautiful German girl was drinking close by. Suddenly she stood up and walked over to Ustinov. "Well, I guess I win my bet." She said.

"Your bet? I'm sorry; I don't know what you mean," replied a flustered Ustinov.

"Oohh, that's what I swore would happen, and you promised me it wouldn't."

By now Ustinov was completely vexed. "Look, I really don't know what you're talking about."

"That night, which I shall never forget, in bed you said to me it was one of the most important nights of your life, and you said you had to go back to your wife and family, which I understand. After all, I'm only a prostitute, but you said you'd never forget me, and I said, oh yes you will. Like all men you will forget me. Well, I win my bet, don't I?"

"No," Ustinov managed to spurt out. "You don't, because I don't remember any of this."

"Well, then, let me tell you something. You are not a very honourable man, Mr James Robertson Justice."[2]

Ustinov later regaled Justice with this treasured incident. "Oh Christ!" he blustered. "Well, thank you anyway."[3]

There was another curious case of mistaken identity concerning Justice some years later. In February 1962, Justice was wanted in Denmark for charges of fraud and embezzlement. This was of course a case of mistaken identity, but at the time was cause for some concern. For several weeks, a confidence trickster (posing as an English eccentric, Lancelot Spratt type character and bearing an uncanny resemblance to Justice) worked his way through Copenhagen, tricking various organisations out of a huge amount of money. As the resemblance became apparent, rumours started to go round that this chap was in-fact the famous British actor – and as they gathered pace, the Danish press started to publish photos of Justice as the wanted man! After a few phone calls from the British Consulate in Copenhagen the mistake was explained and Justice received an apology. However, to this day nobody knows what happened to the trickster.[3]

Despite an interesting cast, that included Roger Livesey and a fourteen year old Anthony Newley as the body-swapping father and son, Vice Versa was a box-office flop. At least things worked out for Justice, whose turn as the son's fearsome headmaster, Dr. Grimstone, won him a contract with Rank. For years afterwards Justice acknowledged Ustinov for having set him on the path to a successful screen career. "I was dragged into the film world, more or less by the scruff of the neck," he explained in a TV interview, "by the son of a former colleague of mine, a man called Peter Ustinov. He more or less pulled me into the trade and I've had a very good time in it."[4]

Justice's next substantial film, *Scott of the Antarctic* (1948) was a highly prestigious affair indeed. Because of his close links with Peter Scott, Justice was particularly keen to be involved in a film that celebrated the exploits of his friends' famous father, even to the point of sacrificing his beard, having it shaved off for the early sequences, though his famous whiskers return as the doomed expedition nears the South Pole. Even this early in his career, the Justice whiskers were becoming something of a trademark. Asked by a friend why he grew a beard and maintained one, he said: "It gives me an extra 10 minutes in bed in the morning. I think scraping your face every day is an absurd business.[5]

There is something intensely British about great heroism that ends in abject failure and the story of Robert Falcon Scott personifies it totally. Critic Kenneth Halliwell called the film, 'the stiff-upper-lip saga par excellence'[6] Already a famed polar explorer, Scott set out in 1910 to reach the South Pole. It took two years for his small party to reach it only to discover a Norwegian flag planted by Roald Amundsen flying there. On the way back the entire party perished in the snows, and when Scott's diaries were found by a search team several months later his daring battle against insurmountable odds thrilled the whole of Edwardian England.

After the Second World War, Ealing's name had become synonymous with comedy, but *Scott of the Antarctic* was to be one of the studio's more dramatic efforts and an incredible creative team was assembled to tell this stirring tale. The direction was by Charles Frend who had been responsible for the wartime story of epic heroism, *San Demetrio, London*. While the Technicolor cinematography, which had an almost documentary feel to it, was courtesy of Jack Cardiff and Geoffrey Unsworth. The final touch to enhance the picture's prestige was the memorably bleak, desolate score by Ralph Vaughan Williams, one of the composer's rare and most successful forays into film music.

The cast, too, had more stiff upper lips on display than a Dunkirk remembrance service. John Mills played Scott, a popular choice as he had already established his reputation portraying urbane men of courage, and he was ably supported by Kenneth More, John Gregson and a young Christopher Lee.

Justice's role was that of Petty Officer Edgar 'Taff' Evans. It may not have been the largest role Justice ever undertook, but it turned out to be amongst the most challenging due largely to the fact that he very much identified with his character according to friend Keith Shackleton, who visited Justice on the set with two colleagues who were acting as technical advisors. "I remember he found playing 'Taff' Evans extremely emotionally challenging. In fact if I remember rightly he couldn't actually bring himself to watch the film."[7] That Justice was a close friend of Robert Falcon Scott's son obviously added piquancy.

This strong emotional connection with the character is perhaps why Justice was to give arguably his most naturalistic screen performance, and it's quite compelling to watch. Here he demonstrates his ability to combine his more light-hearted performances of the future with real pathos. The subtle, slow disintegration of 'Taff' Evans, described by Scott as the expedition's "tower of strength," as he begins the downward spiral, the first of the party to fall, is truly dramatic.

Mentally challenging, the film was also physically arduous with location work out in Norway and Switzerland. In addition to many hazardous scenes filmed at Ealing on a sound stage covered in 'fuff', as the revolting artificial snow was called.

Chosen as the Royal Command Performance film of 1948, *Scott of the Antarctic* is today deemed a minor classic of British filmmaking, even if its stiff upper lip heroics have sadly rendered it something of a museum piece.

Thanks to *Vice Versa* and *Scott of the Antarctic* Justice was quickly earning a reputation as a supporting player of some quality and highly in demand too, but he had yet to truly find a vehicle to properly exploit the unique screen persona he was beginning to establish. *Poet's Pub* (1949), based on the whimsical novel by Eric Linklater, was another lost opportunity. Although inhabited by some well-known comic players, including Joyce Grenfell, Derek Bond and Justice himself, the film was a disappointment. Neither the critics nor the public liked it, and it sunk without trace.

Some compensation arrived in the form of a close friendship with Linklater. He and Justice spent many an evening drinking, laughing and talking endlessly. "If you can imagine two men with rapier-sharp points to their toes doing a sword-dance, with one of them occasionally letting off a revolver, then you'll have a fair idea of those conversations," wrote Michael Parnell in his 1984 biography of Linklater. "Either Eric or James would introduce a topic and then they'd pursue it hotly, up comic hill and down erudite dale, until the whole party was so exhausted with laughter and surprise that nothing would revive them — except perhaps another glass of Glenmorangie whisky."[8]

Justice's good friend Martin Leslie recalls these verbal jousts: "Eric and James got on very well together, sharing a rude and robust sense of humour and a great ability to express themselves through an amazing use of language. They often argued – sometimes quite heatedly – with neither giving way to the other. Anyone attempting to get involved drew fire from both of them and, if wise, retreated![9]

Another evening saw the two men playing croquet at Linklater's home until it was too dark to see the next hoop. "Eric, who was my partner, kept altering the rules," recalled one of the other guests that day, Ursula Balfour, "but my husband and James Robertson Justice were formidable opponents. Marjorie, Eric's wife, kept pleading with us to go and eat the excellent dinner which was getting cold. Eric and James were old friends and sparring partners. Both were intensely well-informed and that evening they reminded us of two small boys trying to get the better of each other. I don't need to tell you how much Eric enjoyed a convivial evening."[10]

Like the majority of Justice's friends, Linklater was an extraordinary individual; it seems that Justice never bothered seeking out the comradeship of 'normal' people. Although born in Penarth, Wales, in 1899, Linklater spent much of his childhood in Orkney and always considered himself an Orcadian; not unlike Justice himself, born outside of Scotland, but forever considering himself Scottish. Linklater's studies as a medical student were interrupted by nightmarish service as a sniper with the Black Watch in World War One. After the War, he took up journalism, and went on to write twenty three novels. During World War Two, he worked for the War Office recording the Italian Campaign, rediscovering the hidden art treasures of Florence. His anti-war comedy *Private Angelo,* about an Italian deserter who finally finds courage, is one of the finest novels of the War. Peter Ustinov made it into a film in 1949, again with an appearance from Justice.

[1] Ustinov, Peter *'Dear Me'* (Book Club Associates 1979), p 202

[2] Miller, John *'Peter Ustinov, The Gift of Laughter'* (Orion 2003), p 62

[3] The Daily Mail, 9th February 1962

[4] Interview with Joan Bakewell – BBC Television – 1966 – last shown in 2004 as part of BBC4's 1960's season.

[5] Picture Show and TV Mirror, 16th April 1960

[6] Halliwell, Leslie *'Halliwell's Film Guide'* Scribner Book Company (Mar 1989)

[7] Author interview with Keith Shackleton, September 2004

[8] Parnell, Michael *Eric Linklater: A Critical Biography* (John Murray – 1984)

[9] Author interview with Martin Leslie, Isle of Skye, 2007

[10] Ibid

A sketch of JRJ by Anthony Wysard, a founder member of the infamous Thursday Club, circa 1955

CHAPTER 8:
THE THURSDAY CLUB

For Justice, sharing the good things in life with fellow minded friends was an important part of his social outlook. Nowhere was this better exemplified than the notorious lunching group named The Thursday Club, which met once a month in an upstairs room at Wheeler's Restaurant in Old Compton Street, until recently the flagship of the famous restaurant chain that specialises in fish. Regularly denounced by gossip columnists as a focus of all manner of misbehaviour, the purpose of the club was purely convivial: an excuse to start the weekend early, eat Wheeler's finest fish dishes and drink Wheeler's cheap-and-cheerful house white wine – and plenty of it. It was an exclusively male environment, and many wives and girlfriends of the members had long ago reluctantly given up Thursday night as a lost cause.

The club started life in the late 1940s and had as its members, writers, film directors, journalists, actors and politicians, but perhaps most notably Prince Philip. Justice had been introduced to Prince Philip by his Equerry, (and fellow Thursday Club member) the late Commander Michael Parker. They quickly struck up a firm friendship, no doubt built upon their mutual interest in nature and remained friends for many years. Other regulars at The Thursday Club included Baron, the famous society photographer, the Marques of Milford Haven, actors Orson Welles, Peter Ustinov and David Niven, artist Vasco Lazzolo, Arthur Christiansen, perhaps the most famous Daily Express editor, the eminent scriptwriter T.E.B Clark, Lord Glenavy (better known as the stammering raconteur and columnist, Patrick Campbell), the Cabinet Minister Iain Macleod, and other luminaries such as the editors of Tatler and Punch.[1] For a club where things were high-spirited and occasionally raucous, Justice was a devoted member.

In-between courses and bottles of wine, the latest bit of high society gossip was traded for a salacious tall tale or bit of banter. It was all very jolly and informal, totally private, and everyone knew they could relax because nothing said within those panelled walls would ever get into the papers. And if anyone ever became the slightest bit pompous, the rest of the group would all burst out into a spontaneous rendering of 'Lloyd George Knew My Father', which invariably had the desired effect of causing them to subside immediately.[2]

Each week a member was obliged to invite a celebrity along for lunch. One time the famous musician Larry Adler invited the Hollywood actor Rod Steiger as his personal guest. "Mr Steiger happens to be a marvellous actor – but he knows it," Adler wrote later in his autobiography. "He arrived in dark glasses, insisted on keeping them on, and started getting into his Method mode, declaiming from the head of the table as if he was striding the battlements at Elsinore. We got the distinct impression he was expecting everyone to ask for his autograph. At a signal from Christiansen we all burst into song – and Mr. Steiger became a human being again. Cruel? Not really. Just fun. And afterwards I had to write in the club book one hundred times: 'I will not bring Rod Steiger here again.'"[3]

Topics of discussion would often get quite heated at The Thursday Club. On one occasion Larry Adler was on his soapbox about public schools, which he maintained were factories for manufacturing homosexuals. Justice was sitting between Prince Philip and Adler. "Oh Christ, Adler," he boomed. "Are you on that dreary hobby-horse of yours again?"

"Well, it's true," Adler said.

"Of course it's true," said Justice in his foghorn tones. "I went to public school, and I was buggered in my first week there, in the dormitory with all the others watching. It did me no harm whatsoever."

"Jimmy," Adler said. "It was different in those days. The whole school had to turn out to watch because of their motto: 'Justice must not only be done, but must be seen to be done'

The whole table exploded in laughter. "I thought Prince Philip was going to fall off his chair," Adler later recalled.[4]

Pranks were sometimes the order of the day. The meeting place was a private room opposite what is now the Prince Edward Theatre but in those days was

The London Casino. The members sat at one long table under a sea-green ceiling, and there was a cuckoo clock on the wall above the fireplace behind the chair at the head of the table. Predictably, on the hour and half-hour a cuckoo would emerge, but its appearances on the half-hour were fleeting to say the least. One day, by way of an amusing wager, the club members bet Baron that he would not be quick enough to take a snapshot of the cuckoo when it popped out at half past one. Baron rose to the challenge – and failed. Next week, he tried again – setting his camera on a tripod, but no luck. A member nudged his arm at the vital moment. At the third attempt, Baron insisted that none of the club members be allowed within touching distance of him. But this didn't stop the pranksters; one of them came armed with three thunder-flashes – small, safe, and lightly-explosive smoke bombs, used in military training. Just as the hands of the cuckoo clock reached half past one, Justice and Prince Philip deployed the thunder-flashes: one burst immediately under Baron's camera, one landed on a table and the third ended up in the fireplace, where its explosion prompted a downfall of soot from the chimney. The place erupted with laughter, quelled somewhat when the police arrived, and a general consensus was reached that it was perhaps time to call off the wager.[5]

It was because of The Thursday Club that Justice became acquainted with Helen Courtney Lewis, who together with three other girls shared a flat on the Kensington/Chelsea border. "We knew him," says Helen, "and many of his escapades, one might say *intimately*, one of us in the biblical sense of the word"[6]

Helen's closest friend was Bette. "She and I were the two 'do it all devils' whose motto was: 'fun at all costs.' Bette was secretary to Baron, and got to know Justice intimately. Though Justice was still married, indeed Dilys had given birth to a son, christened James, in 1945, both of them found the time and the place, as it were. The place being for the most part the girl's flat in Kensington. "James was a giant of a man," recalls Helen. "With generous girth, a voice that matched and a large ginger beard, while Bette was tiny, only about 5ft tall and no beauty. She had, however, the charm of a Bridget Jones, wacky and helpless. A favourite performance of James' was divesting himself of his upper and outer garments and with only a sporran to hide his assets, would walk round the flat playing the bagpipes. I can honestly say I saw more of James' bum than the rest of him."[7]

After some time Bette married and left for Germany where her husband was an officer in the army of occupation, but returned after only three weeks of married life to the welcoming arms of Justice. So once again the actor became a regular visitor to the flat. "One night," remembers Helen, "my other flat mates and I decided to attach a Swiss cow bell to the bed. That night as usual James and Bette returned home reaching the third floor in the creaking lift, both the worse for wear. Ours was an action we all regretted as it kept us awake nearly all night. Next morning when I surfaced with the hopes of taking a bath, I found that James had beaten me to it and was lying in the bath with a cigar in one hand and a copy of the Tatler in the other hand. Bubbles arose from the water in a constant melodious, if malodorous stream. Poor Bette, obviously worn out, was outside in the corridor on all fours with an eiderdown draped over herself while clutching a bowl of cornflakes which she was attempting to spoon down an unwilling throat."[8]

Bette, with her thirtieth birthday well behind her was beginning to feel broody; half hoping Justice would consent to become the father to a child. But her predilection to alcohol dashed all hopes. But there is no doubt that their attachment was more than just physical as they remained close friends for more than three years. Slowly and inevitably, though, they both went their separate ways. Bette died in 2006 at the age of 83. "Two lives, so different," stresses Helen. "I miss them both."

[1] Adler, Larry *'Me & My Big Mouth'* (Blake Publishing – 1994), p125 & 126

[2] Ibid., p126

[3] Ibid., p127

[4] Ibid., p128

[5] Ibid., p129

[6] Correspondence to author from Helen Courtney Lewis – 2006

[7] Ibid

[8] Ibid

CHAPTER 9:
WHISKY GALORE!

Justice's career received a massive boost in 1949 when he appeared in his first bona fide classic comedy movie *Whisky Galore*, the adaptation of Compton Mackenzie's fictionalised account of a true event; that of a shipwreck looted of its cargo of whisky.

More importantly, cast as Dr. Maclaren, the island's doctor, Justice began to develop the on-screen persona that had begun in *Vice Versa*. His performance as the doctor is pivotal, being at once an authority figure but whose true allegiance is with his patients – and the island as a whole. As the title of the film suggests, whisky to the islanders is more than a mere beverage, but the water of life itself. Dr. Maclaren illustrates its health-giving properties, prescribing it to a bed-ridden patient, old Hector. As the old man enjoys the rejuvenating qualities of a glass of whisky, his doctor joins him in a dram, too, of course! When Gordon Jackson's character, George Campbell, decides to stand up to his cantankerous widowed mother's wishes, and marry his girlfriend, Dr. Maclaren is there to administer a glass of whisky – for extra courage.

In fact the whole film can be seen as a homage to the restorative powers of Scotch, which magically restores a community in deep depression for want of a wee dram. Producer Monja Danischewsky called the film: "The longest unsponsored advertisement ever to reach cinema screens the world over."[1]

The story was based on a real-life incident that occurred in 1941 on the Hebridean island of Eriskay when the SS Politician ran aground with a cargo that included 22,000 cases of whisky. Dozens of boats from every nearby island soon set upon the wreck, rescuing some 7,000 cases from a watery end, and their tale quickly became legend. It was perfect subject matter for Ealing, a studio already turning out subversive little comedies. Their stories of the little man battling to overcome the powers of Establishment hit a nerve with a British people still reeling from the effects of war. Community and the strength of its individuals is the heart that beats at the centre of many of Ealing' finest films and authority is there to be made fun of. But there's warmth and humanity running beneath the subversion. Few of Ealing's comedies are a better example of this than *Whisky Galore*, focusing on the clash between the locals and the island's forces of authority, led by the pompous English Home Guard Commander (Basil Radford) who is determined to protect the cargo at all costs. Look out too for writer (and good friend of JRJ) Compton Mackenzie, who makes a cameo appearance in the film as Captain Buncher.

Justice's involvement in the film went deeper than merely acting and allowing him to use his beloved Scottish accent. His contract stated that he was also hired "on script work… advising on local casting and locations."[2] Shot on the island of Barra, the production was beset by often appalling weather which made things difficult for its debut director, the American born Alexander Mackendrick, who would make other classic Ealing comedies *The Man in the White Suit* and *The Lady Killers*. But the film's success owes much to its remarkable feeling of authenticity; most of the extras came from among the islanders living nearby.

After a slow start at the English box-office, *Whisky Galore* became a worldwide hit and Ealing's most profitable film. In America censors insisted on a coda being inserted at the end of the film stating that the stolen whisky brought nothing but unhappiness to the islanders; even though quite the opposite was true in real life.

The second of three films Ealing released in 1949, the others being *Passport to Pimlico* and *Kind Hearts and Coronets*, the enormous success of *Whisky Galore* helped forever link 'Ealing' and 'comedy' in the public imagination. It even spawned a sequel in 1957. Called *Rockets Galore*, it was based on another Compton Mackenzie story and focused this time on the islanders attempts to prevent the RAF building a rocket base. Despite a good cast, including Donald Sinden, Gordon Jackson and Ronnie Corbett, the film failed to match its illustrious predecessor.

Indeed such was the success of the original that Compton Mackenzie and Justice discussed the possibility of forming their own production company, Albyn Films, based in Scotland. Moray Maclearn, the historian, and novelist Eric Linklater were also members of this group. It was hoped a combination of government money and private investors would kick start the company, with most of the money and films being made in Scotland. The first production planned was a light comedy, to be followed by an adaptation of a Sir Walter Scott story. Alas, the daring scheme never materialised.[3]

As an amusing footnote, 14 whisky bottles said to be the last surviving from the wreck of the SS Politician, the real-life shipwreck that inspired the film, were sold in 1993 at a Glasgow auction for £12,012, with a bottle of Haig Dimple fetching £1,210.[4]

[1] Duguid, Mark 'Whisky Galore!' – Screenonline.co.uk

[2] McArthur, Colin *'Whisky Galore! & The Maggie'* (I B Tauris & Co – 2002)

[3] Moss, Norman, *'Little John, has a big appetite – For Life!'* (Picturegoer Magazine – April 19th 1952) p 14

[4] Halliwell, Leslie *'Halliwell's Film Guide'* Scribner Book Company (Mar 1989)

JRJ fishing outside his home in the late 1940's, not long before his son's tragic death.

CHAPTER 10:
TRAGEDY

While enjoying deserved success in the cinema, Justice faced a family tragedy of unimaginable horror when his young son, James Norval Robertson Justice, died in a drowning accident at home. Home at the time was Falling Mill House, a 400 year old building in the tiny Hampshire village of Whitchurch, a beautiful location that held for the family previously happy memories.[1]

The converted mill sat beside a deep, fast-flowing river and Justice built a step down to the water as it exits from under the mill in order that he could go for a swim every morning, summer and winter, in the mill tail, in spite of the often freezing temperatures. He also went hawking in the area, using a small car to transport his birds. It had a pole across the back seat for them to perch on and a roll back canvas sunroof. Because the car was too small for him, Justice had to drive it with his head stuck out of the top.[2]

During one summer Justice noticed that the weed in the river needed drastic attention and thinking that using a scythe was too much like hard work he took a Allen Scythe, a motorised grass cutter, up the river, tied two old oil drums to it for buoyancy, put it in the water and started to cut the weed, very effectively by all accounts. As he worked his way down stream he noticed the water level was getting very high so he got out and walked down to the mill and saw that he had sent down so much weed that the hatches were all blocked solid. "He decided to see if he could get some help from local people he knew that either

Left: James' only child, James Norval in 1948, about a year before his tragic death. (Jamie Tompson) Right: JRJ and friend, in the garden of his home at Whitchurch in the late 1940's.

worked on the river or around it but they all told him none too politely to go away," says Chas House, who works today as the River Keeper on the River Test in Whitchurch. "But one man told him to go round to Ken Jones' house who had worked on the river all his life. Justice went round and knocked on his door, Ken opened it and when Justice explained what had happened Ken told him he was a complete moron and that he would come and have a look after he had finished his Sunday lunch and to sod off till then."[3]

When Ken Jones arrived very little water could get through the hatches and the weed was backed thirty yards up stream. Jones was able to get in and stand on the mass of weeds and cut it into blocks and push it through the hatches with his foot. "He did not finish until 8pm that night," recalls Chas House. "Justice then asked him if he could look after that stretch from then on. Ken said yes on condition that he did not interfere and bloody well left alone things he knew nothing about!!"[4]

Justice's son had begun to make friends in the town, one of which had been a new arrival just like himself. Michael Codd, now an artist based in Hampshire, remembers being evacuated during the Second World War from Wembley in London to the relative serenity of Whitchurch. Codd's house had been fairly close to the huge Park Royal Industrial Estate in Acton which was a prime strategic target for the Luftwaffe.[5]

His mother, Iris Lovell, had been born in Whitchurch and it was an ideal place to return to as her father still ran the small village's barber shop there. Situated in the Square at the heart of Whitchurch, Paul Lovell's barber shop looked after the locals but also had some unusual customers, many of whom came from the nearby prisoner of war camp. Michael Codd well recalls that the men were German and Italian officers and much to a young boy's delight, always accompanied by an armed British soldier who would sit smoking and chatting whilst the POWs had their hair cut.[6]

Codd's family came back to stay in Whitchurch during the summer holidays for several years after the war and it was during this time that he came to know little James Robertson Justice, whose father chose the local barber shop to have his hair cut. This was a delight for Codd's mother as she was a very keen autograph hunter. In an era when the movie industry still had no rivals Iris found a customer who was acting in British, and occasionally American, films and was generous enough to ask his fellow actors to sign her autograph book. Iris was delighted, for instance, when Justice came back from making *Captain Horatio Hornblower RN* with the autographs of Virginia Mayo and Gregory Peck.[7]

James Robertson Justice soon noticed Iris' son Michael around the shop and suggested that he should come to play with his son at The Mill. As they were similar ages, this worked out very well, and Codd remembers the lovely teas that were served there. Tragically, this friendship was to be all too brief when Iris had to tell her son that he wouldn't be able to go to the mill again as young James had drowned in the river.[8]

Justice had always warned his son never to play on his own near the river that ran through the grounds of the house. When the boy started toddling into the garden, Dilys suggested a fence to keep the child safe from the water. James wouldn't hear of it. Any child of his must learn to live with the elements, as he had done himself, he insisted. The inevitable happened on the Monday evening of 20th June 1949. The family had just returned from a weekend's holiday, and little James, then just four-years-old, went off fishing for minnows in the river with two playmates, Eric Dunlop and Lincoln McKrill, both aged ten. The two older boys fished without success for some ten minutes before noticing that little James was missing and began a frantic search around the mill. In a panic they rushed to inform Justice who ran at once to the river and found his son's body floating face downwards under the mill by some weeds. Using a weed rake Justice pulled his son out and despite

As Arthur Peters in 'Stop Press Girl' with Joyce Barbour, 1949

every effort to save him, artificial respiration and stimulants, little James was dead within the hour.[9]

An inquest was held at Whitchurch on the following Wednesday where the two boys gave evidence, along with the local physician, Dr R. H. Walker, who said that he saw the deceased at about 7pm and applied artificial respiration for a considerable while without success. The Deputy Coroner for Hampshire, Mr T.G. Royatt, returned a verdict of "accidental death due to drowning" and expressed his deep sympathy with the child's parents.[10]

Justice was devastated and unsurprisingly was never quite the same man again; it more or less destroyed him with guilt. Was this guilt due to the fact that, according to another account, Justice had failed to teach his son to swim despite the close proximity of the mill house to the weir?

The tragedy also had a profound effect on Justice's marriage according to Keith Shackleton. "It was mainly due to the death of their son that their marriage collapsed. It was tragic for all concerned but I think that Dilys found it very difficult to forgive James and that of course put enormous pressure on them."[11]

The tragedy of his son's downing never left Justice. How could it? Years later, when his good friend Martin Leslie was staying at Spinningdale, Justice asked if he could go to his room and collect a book for him. "I went along to his room and I couldn't immediately find it. He came eventually to see why it was taking so long. I'd just found it, and on his bedside-table was a little, framed drawing of a child's head, which was done by Peter Scott. I asked him who it was. He said: 'Oh, that's my son.' He then told me about young James and said that he'd died in a drowning accident. I think it was Phillip Glasier who told me that he thought that had been the beginning of the end as far as Dilys was concerned. Anyway, he said: 'I don't talk about it.' And so the matter was never discussed again."[12]

[1] Email from Chas House (September 2005) – courtesy of Roy McKie

[2] Ibid

[3] Ibid

[4] Ibid

[5] Email from Mike Codd (June 2007) – courtesy of Mark Fenton

[6] Ibid

[7] Ibid

[8] Ibid

[9] Hampshire Chronicle, 25th July 1949

[10] Official coroner's report

[11] Author interview with Keith Shackleton, September 2004

[12] Author interview with Martin Leslie, Isle of Skye, 2007

As 'Red Dougal' in 'Anne of the Indies', 1951

CHAPTER 11:
A MATTER OF POLITICS

One of the most intriguing aspects of Justice's personality was the contradiction surrounding his political motivations. As mentioned earlier, Justice had fought for The International Brigade against the fascists in the Spanish Civil War. He was a staunch socialist, celebrating the 1945 Labour election victory in the pubs of Wigtown.[1] However, in his social habits he was as far removed from socialism as could be imagined. His interests revolved round falconry, wildfowling and fishing and most of his socialising took place in the conservative drawing rooms of large country houses. He was a good friend of Prince Philip and later introduced the young Prince of Wales to the art of falconry.

He was perhaps the original champagne socialist, that somewhat derisory term for those Labour supporters of a theatrical bent. According to Sir Peter Scott's biographer, Elspeth Huxley, Justice was "indifferent to money" and that when he gave a party at London's Wheeler's restaurant, home of The Thursday Club, "the caviar was served in pudding bowls and the guests helped themselves with table spoons."[2]

Nevertheless Justice put his political money where his mouth was and stood as Labour candidate in the 1950 General Election for North Angus and Mearns, a seat in Northeast Scotland, a part of Aberdeenshire; a nice family connection being the fact that his father had been born in Aberdeen.[3] The fact that his candidacy was funded by the local constituency party, rather than one of the

Dilys Justice, James' first wife presenting prizes at an agricultural show in the early 1950's (Jamie Tompson)

unions, indicated that they considered it highly unlikely that he had any chance of winning in such a strongly Conservative territory. Justice had been a Labour Party agent for Galloway in 1945 so must have realised that the chance of an upset was slim. And so it proved. Justice polled over eight thousand votes, but his Conservative rival took twice as many votes. After the Labour landslide of 1945, Winston Churchill and the Conservative Party were now restored to power and Justice resumed his acting career, his brief dream of becoming a Member of Parliament dashed against the rocks of reality.

Years later in a television interview with Joan Bakewell, Justice was asked if it was his reputation for being angered by much in modern life, his railing against certain British institutions that propelled him to stand for Parliament. "No not anger," he replied. "Except unless you say all forms of political consciousness must be dictated to a certain extent by anger. Do you get angry if you think of injustices? Well of course you do. You get angry if you see a child being ill-treated. It's a question of degree." Becoming a candidate, Bakewell presumed, was a chance to do something about such things. "I've had certain advantages other people have not," Justice carried on, "and I wanted to put something back again. I'm still an unrepentant socialist and I imagine always will be."[4]

When Justice ran on the Labour ticket in the General Election of 1950 and stood as a candidate for Parliament, "and hopefully a member but of course it didn't get that far"[5] he had a special clause in his movie contract that allowed him to do so. More bizarrely, he had a film coming out at the same time as the election and so had to employ a pseudonym. He chose – Seumas Mor na Feusaig. An odd choice of pseudonym one might think, though Seumas Mor na Feusaig may have been more than mere affectation, as the seat he was hoping to win at the time still had a significant proportion of Gaelic speakers. A literal translation of Justice's cinematic nom de plume is Big James of the Beard.

The film in question was *The Magnet* (1950), pretty well forgotten today save for it being the starring debut of a child actor called William Fox, who grew up, changed his name to James Fox and subsequently enjoyed a distinguished film career (*The Servant*, *Performance*). Fox played the ten-year-old son of a psychiatrist, who acquires the magnet of the film's title, believing it to be a good-luck token, and convinced that he will be arrested for the crime, flees his home. On his misadventures he encounters a gang of youths, as well as a tramp, played by Justice, who enjoyed the opportunity the project afforded to be reunited with Charles Frend, the director with whom he had worked on *Scott of the Antarctic*.

Despite its pleasing setting of a post-war, pre-Beatles Liverpool, *The Magnet* is a curiously charmless film and not up to scratch with other Ealing productions of the period, even though it derives from the not inconsiderably talented Tibby Clarke (a fellow member of The Thursday Club), who wrote the screenplays for *Passport to Pimlico* and *The Blue Lamp*, which featured a young and relatively unknown actor called Dirk Bogarde.

Much better was *The Black Rose* (1950) a vehicle for one of Hollywood's greatest romantic leads and swashbucklers, Tyrone Power, though he was by now looking a bit long in the tooth to play a young 13th-century Saxon nobleman who, after sparking an unsuccessful rebellion against the Norman conquerors of his homeland, sets out to seek his fortune in the Far East. It's all rather an odd mix of Robin Hood, Ivanhoe and Marco Polo, but divertingly pleasing in a Saturday morning pictures sort of way. Orson Welles' charismatic Mongol warlord, that owes something to his screen portrayal of Macbeth of just a few years before, and Jack Cardiff's exquisite Technicolor camerawork deserve special mention.

Justice makes only a few appearances at the beginning of the film and sadly missed out on location filming in Morocco, but is in good company with fellow players of the stature of Michael Rennie and Jack Hawkins. Look closely too for a very early appearance from Lithuanian-born British actor Laurence Harvey, who plays Power's Norman half-brother, a role that Harvey hoped would kick-start his career. He has barely any screen-time and would have to wait several more years before making his mark in British new wave classics like *Room at the Top*.

As the new decade unfolded a cold financial wind blew through the British film industry and Rank, in order to save money, let go many of their contract artists, one of which was Justice. But it didn't seem to faze him, work was coming in now from overseas, such as an offer from 20th Century Fox to go out to Hollywood to appear in *David and Bathsheba* (1951), playing the King's chief lieutenant. This was the first of four films Justice would make with legendary star Gregory Peck, and the two men became firm friends. *David and Bathsheba*, however, is a predictably overblown and stodgy cinematic adaptation of the Old Testament story which sees King David (Peck), hero of his people fall victim to the sins of the flesh when he falls in love with Bathsheba (Susan Hayward), the wife of one of his generals. Cue lots of wrath of God type stuff and battle scenes.

Justice found far better material on his return home when he starred alongside Peck again in the screen adaptation of C.S. Forester's naval hero, *Captain Horatio Hornblower* (1951). This is an entertaining slice of nautical derring-do from veteran Hollywood director Raoul Walsh and there's an uncharacteristic but highly effective turn from Justice as archetype salt-of-the-earth seadog Quist. The film is notable also for giving early roles to the likes of Stanley Baker, Christopher Lee and Richard Johnson.

Another performer whom Justice would appear alongside in several films was the wonderful and quite unique Margaret Rutherford. Quintessentially English, Margaret Rutherford, like Justice, was a late starter in the acting profession. Unlike Justice, though, she had long held an ambition to tread the boards, but was unable to fulfil it until middle age. With her jutting jaw, imperious manner and her no-nonsense approach, she made the perfect foil to Justice, and it's unfortunate that they only made three films together, with *Miss Robin Hood* (1952), a charming little sub-Ealing comedy, being the first of them.

Justice revels in the villainous role of an unscrupulous distiller who cheats Margaret Rutherford's predictably dotty Miss Honey out of a fortune by snatching a winning whisky formula that has been the property of her family for generations. Maggie retaliates with an Entebbe-style raid on Justice's premises, aided by shy newspaper writer Richard Hearne, creator of a comic strip character called Miss Robin Hood. As the name suggests, the character is a female re-working of the Robin Hood legend in which the heroine robs banks, with the assistance of a gang of teenage girls and then redistributes the wealth.

The supporting cast list reads like a 'Who's Who' of British screen comedy of the time; Dora Bryan, Peter Jones, Sid James, Reg Varney, Kenneth Connor

Putting on a brave face – Dilys & JRJ attend a social engagement in 1950, just a year after the tragic death of their son, James. (Jamie Tompson)

and Michael Medwin. As for its director John Guillermin, he went on to carve out a successful Hollywood career in the seventies with blockbusters *The Towering Inferno* and *Death on the Nile*.

Comedy may have provided Justice with a steady income, but his on-screen demeanour could just as easily switch to something less benign. And, before he became typecast as everyone's belligerent, if ultimately benign, uncle or father-in-law, he occasionally popped up in more dramatic fair, such was the case in *The Voice of Merrill* (1952) a low budget, but intriguing thriller. As one critic put it, Justice's "crinkly… eyes could suddenly turn very nasty indeed."[6]

Justice plays a successful playwright whose bored glamourous wife has an affair with a failed writer played by Edward Underdown, who may or may not be implicated in the murder of a female blackmailer. Justice here demonstrates his rather underused dramatic abilities and positively shines as an intellectual snob who disdains everything and everybody, stealing the film from under the noses of his fellow players. In one scene, his wife brings up the literary accomplishments of her lover, Justice gives her short shrift: "Don't compare a down-and-out hack with one of the field marshals of English literature." Needless to say, the field marshal, in question, is himself!

Although a quota quickie made for an astonishingly meagre £25,000, John Gilling, directing from his own script turns in a fine little picture. Gilling went on to direct two mid-60s Hammer horror pictures, *The Plague of the Zombies* and *The Reptile*, and here manages to assemble a decent cast, including Valerie Hobson as Justice's unfaithful wife. Hobson's film career was sadly short-lived, but highly productive with appearances in *The Bride of Frankenstein*, *Great Expectations* and *Kind Hearts and Coronets* before she retired from show business upon marrying MP John Profumo. After her husbands 'scandal,' following revelations about his relationship with call girl Christine Keeler, an affair that helped topple the government, Valerie stood by him and they devoted the rest of their lives to charity work.

[1] www.wigtownbookfestival.com

[2] Huxley, Elspeth *'Peter Scott: Painter & Naturalist'* (Faber & Faber 1995)

[3] Torrens, Hugh, *Justice Denied*, Geoscientist Magazine, April 2002

[4] Interview with Joan Bakewell – BBC Television – 1966 – last shown in 2004 as part of BBC4's 1960's season.

[5] Ibid

[6] Picturegoer Magazine – April 19th 1952

CHAPTER 12:
A BRUSH WITH WALT DISNEY

In 1952 Justice was to make the first of a trilogy of historical movies for Walt Disney, Hollywood's master animator, all with the same lead actor – the wonderful Richard Todd, who in the fifties was the epitome of the dashing British leading man. During the Second World War Richard Todd had served with distinction as a paratrooper and his time in the army lent an authenticity to many of his uniformed roles, the most famous portrayal being that of Wing Commander Guy Gibson in the classic British war film *The Dambusters*. Todd first came to international prominence in 1949, earning an Oscar nomination as the dying soldier in *The Hasty Heart*, which also brought him to the attention of Walt Disney.

In 1950, Walt Disney decided to expand his franchise by breaking out into live-action and set up a film crew in England to work on a series of projects. Out of the gate first was the classic *Treasure Island* with Robert Newton's immortal performance as Long John Silver. The second project was one close to Disney's heart, a retelling of the Robin Hood legend. Of course Sherwood Forest had already provided the backdrop for a succession of films about Robin Hood, most famously the 1939 Errol Flynn version, but Walt was determined to make his as historically accurate as possible. Whether he achieved this or not is highly debatable, yet *The Story of Robin Hood and his Merrie Men* remains an entertaining slice of English history – Hollywood style.

One way Disney was determined to be as faithful a possible to the Robin Hood legend was to hire a top British director and cast mainly top English actors. He also wanted to shoot in Sherwood Forest itself, which in the end was not logistically possible. Behind the camera was Ken Annakin, a former documentary maker and veteran of many British movies (including the popular Huggett films) but this would be his first taste of a big budget studio picture; a valuable experience when he went on later to make epics like *Those Magnificent Men In Their Flying Machines*, *The Longest Day* and *Battle of the Bulge*. Annakin was glad to have someone like Todd as his lead, "although he was no acrobatic movie idol like Errol Flynn. He was, in fact, short like Alan Ladd, and often had to be stood on an apple box, or walk on a plank beside Maid Marion, so that one didn't notice the discrepancy in height. But Richard was a good trouper. I remember one scene where he had to swim across the castle moat under fire. I watched the prop man fasten a special cork covered backplate under Dick's shirt and, completely trustful, he jumped into the moat and started swimming. At a signal from me an archer, supposedly the finest in Great Britain, fired an arrow. It stuck in Robin's back and he rolled over apparently mortally injured as planned, but when I cut the shot and they pulled Dick out of the water, it was found that the barb was sticking precariously right on the edge of the cork. Another quarter of an inch to the right and there would have been no more acting for Dick."[1]

Annakin would work many times with both Todd and Justice in the future but it was here at Denham Studios where their paths first crossed. Annakin remembered Justice as, "a mountain of a man. He was a natural extrovert with great energy, a loud voice and a treble ration of humour."[2]

Not surprisingly, given his ample girth and proclivity to merry making, Justice had been cast as Little John. The famous quarter-staff duel between Little John and Robin, a highlight of any Robin Hood film, took three weeks to rehearse with stuntman Rupert Evans, an expert sword-master and fight arranger. A wooden bridge was built over a tank of water in the studio and as is usual with such things not everything went according to plan. After a few playful bashes, Todd was knocked into the water as rehearsed, and Justice jumped in after him. Without a pause they continued to parry and thrust, as choreographed, until Todd stepped on a nail that penetrated his thin deerskin boot. "Shit!," he yelled and losing his balance accidentally swiped Justice a mighty blow across the head. With a cry of, "foul, not fair," Justice disappeared beneath the water, only to reappear, angry and sputtering, but still in character: "Varlet!" he cried. "Have you no respect for the pate of a philosopher? If you've damaged the old brain box, Scotland would loose one of its finest minds"[3]

JRJ and Richard Todd, hands on hips looking extremely menacing in 'The Story of Robin Hood and his Merrie Men' – 1952

Justice had first won Todd's admiration at an earlier script conference. "Like me, James Robertson Justice was a countryman," Todd remembers. "And we shared a love of field sports, particularly game shooting and wildfowling. One of his skills was way beyond me: he was a practiced and dedicated falconer and flew various types of raptors. His rural activities took precedence over his more urban pursuits, as, for example, when he parked his car on the forecourt of the Dorchester Hotel and airily instructed a startled doorman to keep an eye on it and its contents. The car was a Rolls-Royce which he had had converted to a shooting-brake and in the back was a squealing litter of piglets!"[4]

Annakin, too, has fond memories of Justice from the films that they made together; particularly he looked forward to lunch time when Justice would regale the whole canteen with stories, usually of the very tall variety. "He'd tell of how he dropped his rifle in front of Hitler when the Germans marched into the Rhine; how he had been forced to flee Arabia on a camel after penetrating a sheik's harem (he said he had been serving as the political advisor to one of the first oil sheiks). These and many other experiences certainly added to the verisimilitude which Jimmy was able to bring to any role."[5]

For the crucial role of the Sheriff of Nottingham, Annakin had cast a young actor newly arrived from Australia – Peter Finch. A protégé of Laurence Olivier, *Robin Hood* would be Finch's first movie. In playing dialogue, Finch brought freshness and a snide threat to the villainous character, without the histrionics of his predecessors in the role. Finch and Annakin became great friends but over the years the director was sad to see how the strain of show business made the star hit the bottle. "He drank in order to cope with theatrical challenges he had never dreamed of in the Outback, or truly prepared himself for. Movie life brought him into contact with beautiful, self-centred, ambitious leading ladies whom he invariably fell for. Apart from his last love, a Jamaican painter, I don't think he was ever as happy as his days in Denham, strutting around the stages as the Sheriff of Nottingham!"[6]

Justice makes an endearing Little John, a wonderful mix of your favourite uncle and Shakespeare's Falstaff (a role that he was born to play, but sadly never did). He certainly manages a much more believable job of it than Alan Hale who had been Flynn's right-hand man in *The Adventures of Robin Hood*. Indeed in Disney's version Justice is so much more than a mere supporting player, but a meaningful character in his own right, towering over the diminutive by comparison Todd. It's a performance to treasure.

The Story of Robin Hood and his Merrie Men was chosen for a Royal premiere in London and was a sizable hit, so much so that Disney didn't waste any time getting messrs Annakin, Todd and Justice signed up for another merrie old England Technicolor romp.

Walt Disney was a man fascinated by the pageantry and history of England and wanted to make a movie about that most colourful of monarchs Henry VIII, but steering well clear of the oft repeated tales of his six wives that had already been done, unmatchably so in the persona of Charles Laughton and the hands of Alexander Korda. Instead *The Sword and the Rose* (1953) focuses on the little known story of Mary Tudor, Henry VIII's sister, who is destined to marry King Louis of France. Naturally, she would much rather wed her true love, Charles Brandon, a commoner (enter stage left a stiff upper lipped Richard Todd). And so the audience is embroiled in the machinations of the English court with all its intrigue and plots.

Despite its failings, *The Sword and the Rose* is colourful, handsomely mounted Disney fare. Historical inaccuracies though won't please scholars and critical reaction to the film, especially from the British press, was less than favourable due to its fidelity to historical truth. The critic for the London Times, however, had to admit that "Mr. James Robertson Justice gives to Henry the gleam of mingled cunning and good nature which may well have peered out of those shrewd Welsh eyes."[7]

Really there was only one actor in the world who could do 'justice' to the role of Henry VIII, and the fact that he bore a heavy resemblance to Holbein's famous portrait of the King added extra dimension to his characterisation. Annakin himself considered Justice "perfect" for the role of the larger than life Tudor monarch and it remains one of the director's favourite characterisations in any of his own films.[8] This is both to the picture's advantage and also a reason for its downfall. Todd and Glynis Johns, playing Mary Tudor, never really convince as lovers and the film is inevitably subsumed by the personality of Justice's Henry VIII. This is the first example of the actor's latter grand scene-stealing at every given opportunity. That his own personality intersected perfectly with the character also laid the groundwork for future roles, including the *Doctor* films' Sir Lancelot.

Justice also shared a common love with Henry VIII in the age old sport of falconry. The actor would often have birds on set – or at least in his dressing room. 'Falcons within – Keep out' was the sign that was affixed to the door of Justice's dressing room at Pinewood studios. It was put up after an incident that involved an unwary cleaner who had entered and disturbed one of his birds. It had attacked her as it protected the rabbit's corpse Justice had just given it before he had returned to the set.[9]

Another victim was renowned actor Trevor Howard. Justice had brought his favourite falcon, a magnificent peregrine named Siubhlach (Gaelic for swift), to

As King Henry VIII in Walt Disney's 'The Sword & The Rose' – 1953

the studios and left it on a large wooden perch in his room. Howard was working on another picture at Pinewood, had already had a few drinks and came prowling around. Finding the door of Justice's room unlocked, he let himself in and understandably alarmed the resting falcon, sending it into panic. The experience terrified Howard who went berserk and rushed out of the room to escape. He stormed into the bar, where he found James holding court.

"You fucking idiot! What the hell are you doing leaving a lethal bird like that in your room?"

Justice merely stated back at him. "What the bloody hell do you mean by going into my room without asking me, you piss-artist?"[10]

Such was his passion for the sport of falconry that Justice refused film work during the month of August, the height of the grouse season, as friend Martin Leslie attests: "He wouldn't work. He was as good as his word, not that I was with him all that often, but in the summertime he definitely gave up the idea of any films and things. He was always up on the moors for the falconry."[11]

David Hancock, the Canadian publisher, recounts a visit to Vancouver where Justice was giving interviews in a hotel. Between interviews, he would pop next door to chat to Hancock and the great American falconer Frank Beebe. It is a great demonstration of Justice's love of falconry that he would much rather talk about hawking than his latest acting role. Even filming on location, Justice rarely allowed the work to get in the way of some bit of bird business. Dirk Bogarde's 1957 adventure drama *Campbell's Kingdom*, for example, was set in the Canadian Rockies but due to budgetary restraints was shot instead in Italy on the Dolomites. Justice was enthused at the prospect, looking at the various location sites on a map, saying, "Ah, good, we're going up into that ravine, I'll bet we'll see such and such an eagle up there. They're very rare, but I think one should be there." And sure enough it was and his loud bellows of excitement told the whole unit and everyone else in the area that it was the first and only one he'd seen.[12]

Having helped found The Severn Wildfowl Trust with Peter Scott, it seemed odd that Justice also hunted with birds, training falcons to kill other birds. To the uninitiated, hunting and conservation appeared to be very strange bedfellows, but culling as a means to control numbers is a sensible precaution so that one species does not dominate another. With land being at a premium on such a small island as the United Kingdom, some argue that hunting is simply a way of keeping numbers in check. Justice was taken to task on this very topic when interviewed in 1966 by Joan Bakewell. She too found that falconry seemed at odds with bird conservation and the actor's own highly publicised endeavours to save certain species. He replied, quite logically, that in the wild birds kill each other anyway. "It's just nature under command."[13]

"Aren't you aiding and abetting with the sport?" Bakewell argued.

"Well, there's a lot to learn from it," continued Justice, warming to the subject. "The fascination of a falcon's flight, even if it is a bird with a murderous intent. But then again you can say that killing your own food, which thousands of generations have done, is in any way worse than sitting down and eating a steak that someone else has killed for you?" A good argument, one must agree."[14]

Justice took the sport extremely seriously, even training the falcons himself, which could take up to seven months. The training of a falconer might take even longer. Having obtained the bird and retained it in a dark shed until its feathers are adult enough for training, Justice described the three stages of training thus: In the first the birds are taught to strike at a lump of raw meat on the gloved fist of the falconer. In the second they are gradually made to fly while still on a leash to the falconer's fist and to become accustomed to their quarry by the use of a 'lure' made from the wings of the intended prey (often grouse); until the great day when the bird is 'freed' and flies to her master who then teaches her to 'stoop.' The third stage is merely of fully strengthening the 'athletic' endurance of the bird until she can fly and 'stoop' for half an hour on end. She is then ready for taking out, when she is allowed to gorge herself on her first kill. For Justice the joy of the sport lay in the ability of the falconer to master his bird and in the, "intrinsic beauty of the flight of the bird."[15]

In so small a circle of experts it was no surprise that some of the young men Justice befriended went on to become some of the country's leading falconers. One such man is Roger Upton, who has written extensively on the subject, especially on falconry in Arabia, where he's travelled since the sixties. Upton is considered by many to be the principal archivist of the sport of falconry and learnt a great deal from Stephen Frank and from Justice himself. "The first time I met James must have been about 1952," says Upton. "I was only a schoolboy at the time but already a keen Falconer. I knew about James as an actor and as a falconer and decided I wanted to meet him. So I thumbed a lift down to Whitchurch and eventually found him at the Mill. I was terrified but hadn't come all that way for nothing and simply said "Hello, I'm a Falconer." Well we chatted for a while and then I think I started to get on his nerves so eventually left. The next time I saw him was at one of the British Falconry Club meetings. He didn't attend many but when he did he often caused a bit of a stir."[16]

There was also Stephen Frank. Frank had known Justice when he farmed in England, but it was only when they first flew falcons at grouse in 1964 that they became close friends. And they continued hawking together until the actor's death. The moor in Sutherland that Justice rented for his hawking is now owned by Frank. He also lives there in a slightly modernised croft where he flies falcons to this day. He remembers Justice as a good friend and a brilliant raconteur who entertained well.[17]

In 1969 Justice was appointed an honourary member of the British Falconers' Club for his services to a sport which had given him so much pleasure. It was in a way an acknowledgment of the significant part he'd played in the revival of the sport in Britain, after the end of the Second World War.[18]

The Sword and the Rose was the only feature film where Justice appeared with falcons in a professional capacity, and the only role that demonstrated his skill with birds of prey. Justice must also be unique in film history for being the only actor to have employed his personal falcon trainer in a movie. Phillip Glasier, who appeared as Henry VIII's falconer in the film, did for birds of prey what Sir Peter Scott did for waterfowl. He founded what is now the National Birds of Prey Centre, was instrumental in setting up two conservation bodies, wrote three successful books and became one of the world's leading pioneers in breeding birds of prey in captivity at a time when this was thought to be impractical or impossible.

Above all, he had a remarkable affinity with animals and birds, his houses being half-home and half-menagerie, it being no more unusual to find a deer on the landing ("Bloody deer – you know you're not allowed upstairs"), a tawny owl on the top of a door ("Don't shut it or you'll squash his toes") or his faithful pointer, Trudi and a ferret playing on the sofa.[19] Indeed, Glasier had an almost human relationship with animals.

Glasier's love for falconry was bred in him by his beloved step-uncle, Captain Charles Knight, a falconer, wildlife photographer and film-maker, who taught him the art and craft of falconry in his teens.[20] Years later when Glasier was asked to rejoin the British Falconers' Club, to which he had belonged before the Second World War he met Justice at an annual dinner. Justice wanted to see Pru, a hawk Glasier owned, fly; so keen in fact that he drove Glasier in his elderly Rolls-Royce all the way to his home in Hampshire. "I recall that James had a black pointer called Friday, who joined in and wallowed in the reed-beds by the river, pointing moorhens for Pru. Friday was quite a character; he was deaf, or pretended to be. He chased hares as though he was a greyhound and no amount of bellowing on his owner's part would make him desist, but he pointed extremely well. Pru caught a rabbit that Friday had pointed; and when he arrived hot on the scent, he blundered into Pru, who, resenting this, promptly fetched him a smartish swipe across his nose, which surprised him more than somewhat and he never came near her again. He was a large dog, with a great flail of a tail; but he curled himself up in a basket more suited to a toy poodle."[21]

On another occasion Glasier took Pru and a little tiercel called Adolph, over to Justice's home where he was introduced to the Duke of Edinburgh, who had joined the party. "It is on occasions like this that things go wrong," said Glasier. "And that day was no exception. We tried Pru first and hadn't gone more than a few yards when an enormous great hare ran off, ears flat, and its great hind legs pushing along. Pru, who normally avoided such large creatures, evidently had been overcome by our chief guest and shot off after it to grab it. But it was too strong for her, she had a poor hold on it, I got in the way, and the hare made good its escape. Pru flew up into a tree and sat there in a huff, refusing to come down. It was all very embarrassing."[22]

After lunch it was Adolph's turn. "Suddenly he started to chase a green woodpecker which had appeared, rather unwisely, on the scene," recalls Glasier. "As he was gaining on it, James remarked, "God help that woodpecker." The woodpecker, uttering its chippering note, dived into the safety of an oak tree. "James, God has helped that woodpecker," said Prince Philip. We didn't actually lose any hawks and we even caught one rabbit. But it was by no means a good demonstration."[22] In any case Glasier and Justice would fly the two birds at rooks around Winchester, and they were also the falcons used in *The Sword and the Rose*.

There was no flying per se in the Disney film, but there was one scene, Glasier recalls, in which the falcon made her own special contribution. "James, as Henry, was sitting on his throne, feeding the falcon a pigeon's wing. The French ambassador, with retinue, strode up between the ranks of the assembled courtiers, bowed, and made a long and boring speech. During this time the falcon went on plucking feathers out of the wing, taking no notice. The cameras whirred, the lights blazed, sound experts held microphones in strategic places from queer, mechanical crane-like contraptions. The French ambassador ended his speech. There was a pause as Henry drew himself up to reply. Before he could do so the falcon stopped feeding for a moment, looked up, slowly went "Yak, yak, yak," and then continued madly throwing feathers about. It was the perfect reply. Yet for some extraordinary reason it was never used."[23]

Following *The Sword and the Rose* Justice went off to America and came back with an assortment of birds of prey in a zip-bag, causing some consternation at the airport. Walking through customs, his pockets sticky with frozen rat meat which had melted on the way over the Atlantic, he was stopped by officials. "Anything to declare," said the custom's officer.

"Yes, six hawks," replied Justice.

"Six what?"

Justice pulled back the zip-fastener of the bag. The customs man peered inside. Sitting in a row on a perch fitted up in the bag were six hooded birds.

"You'll have to pay duty on those. They're caged birds. They're on the list. How much did you pay for them?"

"I didn't pay anything for them," growled Justice. "I trapped them."

"You what?"

"I caught 'em, chum. Trapped them in a bow-net."

"Where?"

"California."

"All the same, you'll have to pay duty on them."

"Suppose I won't pay any duty," said Justice.

"You've got to."

"No, I haven't. You can keep the hawks."

"Here, you, wait a minute." The customs man called out in alarm as Justice started to walk purposefully out of the customs department, which at Heathrow in the early 1950s pretty much consisted of a shed. "You're not leaving these things here."

"I am, if I have to pay duty on them."

Above: JRJ (left) on a Dabbing expedition with The Duke of Edinburgh (centre) and Prince Charles (third right) in the early 1960's.

Left: A young Prince Charles shows off his catch after an afternoon's 'Dabbing' in the early 1960's

"We've got nothing to feed them."

"I can let you have some rat meat. That's what they ate on the plane." From his pocket Justice produced a bloody mess. The customs man took one horrified look.

"You can take these birds away," he said. "Take 'em away quickly and we won't say any more about it."[24]

Justice went off home triumphant.

The birds in question were a beautiful prairie falcon, a little cooper's hawk, and some tiny western kestrels. He gave Glasier a present of the cooper's hawk and also one of the kestrels. Together the two men enjoyed a few days at Whitchurch with Pru and then took the falcons out after rooks. "It was a day of disaster," Glasier recalls. "James flew a rook over the skyline and the falcon disappeared and, although we searched for hours, we found no trace of her. I flew mine, who put a rook down by a wire fence and then broke her leg on the wire. I carried her home and put her in plaster, but it was an awkward break, the feathers made it extremely difficult to set, and she never recovered. We got James' falcon back the next day. She had chased the rook into a shepherd's hut, where she had been accidentally shut in a few moments after."[25]

Justice and Glasier were once invited by Prince Philip to Sandringham for the day where they flew goshawks at moorhens on the lake. Unfortunately though, Glasiers' hawk failed to put on a decent show for the Royal onlookers. "Pru was a bit uppish to start with too," recalled Glasier. "She missed an easy chance at a rabbit and went off to sulk. I got her back and, rejoining the party, found myself faced with the problem of greeting the Queen in a dignified manner with an irate goshawk bating off my fist."[26]

Not long after that Justice offered Glasier a job. Justice had purchased a house near Inverness, on The Black Isle, and wanted Glasier to look after the place generally and to train and fly falcons for him. Glasier had rubbed shoulders before with film personalities; he once flew falcons for MGM on location with Ava Gardner, Robert Taylor and Stanley Baker. Glasier moved with his family to the north of Scotland, to the Black Isle, and then when Justice bought property near Dornoch, he worked there too, flying falcons for Justice at grouse on a regular basis. One of Phillip Glasier's favourite memories was showing Prince Philip and Prince Charles how he caught flounders in Loch Fleet on the Sutherland coast.[27] This technique (most likely invented by Glasier) is known as 'dabbing' and involves a line of people walking in line through shallow sea pools on a flat sandy shore at low tide. Armed with salmon leisters or pointed sticks, the participants flush out the "dabs" who then swim forward before going back into the sand, where they are occasionally speared, but more often than not escape.

Three years later, without any apparent great ambition but merely a general idea that there should be some sort of centre for falconry and hawking, Glasier moved to Newent in Gloucestershire and set up the Falconry Centre with 12 birds. There were 72 visitors on the first day. From 1967 to 1982, Glasier built the centre to become the world's leading collection of birds of prey with 40,000 visitors a year and, with a great deal of hard work and persistence successfully bred hawks, falcons, eagles, buzzards and owls, becoming a world expert on the subject of captive breeding. Today, renamed the National Birds of Prey Centre, it has the largest collection of birds of prey in the world.[29]

The last of Justice's Disney films with Richard Todd went back to their first for inspiration, *Rob Roy the Highland Rogue* (1954) was a kind of Scottish Robin Hood, a rather stilted version of Sir Walter Scott's classic tale of kilt wearing derring-do. Alas, due to contractual obligations with Rank, Ken Annakin was unable to join them this time and was replaced by Harold French, with whom Justice had worked with on *My Brother Jonathan* (1948).

Richard Todd, of course, played Robert Roy MacGregor, a clan leader in 18th century Scotland attempting to lead his fellow countrymen in a rebellion

As The Duke of Argyll in Walt Disney's, 'Rob Roy, the Highland Rogue', 1953

against the heavy-handed rule of England's King George I, while also romancing and marrying his true love (Glynis Johns, again). Justice plays the Duke of Argyll, a pivotal political manouverer between Todd's rebellious rogue and Michael Gough's traitorous Duke of Montrose.

Filmed in Stirling, soldiers of the Argyll and Sutherland Highlanders, fresh from the conflict in Korea, were recruited for the battle scenes, to double as Redcoats and Rob Roy's men, to lend the film the sort of authenticity the script lacked. French himself summed things up best when he explained to the Queen at the film's Royal performance that it was, "a Western in kilts, Your Majesty."[30] Dilys Powell, the Sunday Times film critic, damned it with faint praise: "To say that this is the best of what Disney calls his all-live action films is, I fear, not saying much, but one must do what small kindnesses one can."[301]

Justice, though, is as watchable as ever, though at one point he's forced to drag up, looking in the words of one critic, "more ill-at-ease than a country curate in a vice raid."[32]

It was on Rob Roy that Justice met Martin Leslie and befriended him. Leslie was one of the Argyll and Sutherland Highlanders roped in as extras for the battle scenes that took two and a half weeks to shoot. On the verge of being de-mobbed Leslie approached the location manager, Alex Bryce and asked that because he wasn't doing anything particular for the next couple of months, could he perhaps stay on. "You ride horses, don't you?" said Bryce. Leslie nodded. "And you've been doing things with the horses in the cavalry charge," continued Bryce, thinking about it. "I could certainly use someone like you. If you look after the horses of the stars, you'll be given the extras' pay of £2 a day, and if you should have to get on a horse for any reason you'll be paid £3 a day. The first thing I'd like you to do is to go now to Dr. Justice's tent (at the time Justice insisted on being addressed as Dr.) where he's just finished a scene and tell him that I've sent you and that you'll be taking-over from Major Boyle to sit on his horse and do the long-shots."[33]

Leslie did what he was told. "I met this man who was a huge fellow sitting on a chair getting his kit off. I told him what I was there for and he said: "Oh good, where do you come from?" I told him I came from Morayshire and he said: "Oh, I live outside Inverness." I got his kit, which was a great deal too big for me but the location manager had told me that I needed his hat, his wig, his coat, and his boots. I went to the wardrobe department who gave me the padding. Feeling somewhat unwieldy once I'd got all this stuff on I went out and got on his beautiful horse. James was the only person I've ever known who galled a horse just by sitting on it. That means it raises a lump which, if you don't watch it, can break. And then you've got problems. I was told that at that stage James weighed something like 18 or 19 stone.[34]

Leslie ended up working on *Rob Roy* for a further six weeks after The Argylls left. "Whilst waiting for his kit he was always full of chat, he was very kind and talked about country matters and wildlife and falcony, which he was clearly very keen on. I had never really seen falconry. He said: "Well, you must come-up and see it. Like anybody else, you get made these invitations from these famous people and you never, ever expect to hear of it again.'"[35]

By now Leslie was put up in the same hotel as the film's stars Richard Todd, Glynis Johns, and Geoffrey Keen. Justice absolutely flatly refused to stay in the same hotel, preferring The Covenanters Arms outside Aberfoyle. Justice was probably the most un-showbiz film actor the business has ever known. He was never seen at the places where film folks were seen. He rarely went to the cinema or indeed the theatre and the majority of his friends were outside the film world. Neither did he feel particularly at home in cities, never spending any more time in them than he could help.[36]

One evening Justice ventured into the hotel where the actors were staying and came into the bar. Leslie was sitting at the far corner of the bar reading a paper. "Where is the boy?' he roared. "Oh, there you are. Come down to my hotel and have a drink. They're an awful stuffy lot here." As Leslie recalls, "James didn't think that much of some of his co-stars in the film. Anyway, I went off down with him to The Covenanters and after that he often asked me down there for a drink, which was great fun. He was a huge presence, things always happened around him and I learnt a great deal. He was also quite keen on the ladies and the landlord of The Covenanters, Robin Steele, was keen on making quite sure that he was never kept short of any supply he might require. I had my eyes opened as a young, wet behind the ears 20 year-old."[37]

When it was time for the film unit to leave Scotland and move back into the studios down south Leslie's contract ended. Before leaving Justice said, "You'll come and see me up north. We'll be in touch." Leslie never, ever expected to hear from Justice again. But there were plenty more adventures to come.[38]

[1] Annakin, Ken 'So You Wanna be a Director?' (Tomahawk Press – 2001) p50

[2] Ibid

[3] Ibid, p51

[4] Author interview with Richard Todd – 2005

[5] Annakin, Ken 'So You Wanna be a Director?' (Tomahawk Press – 2001) p50

[6] Ibid, p57

[7] The Times, date unknown

[8]   Annakin, Ken 'So You Wanna be a Director?' (Tomahawk Press – 2001) p50

[9]   Author interview with Betty Box at Pinewood Studios – 1994

[10]   Phillips, Leslie 'Hello' (Orion – 2006)

[11]   Author interview with Martin Leslie – Isle of Skye – 2007

[12]   Author interview with Betty Box – Pinewood Studios 1993

[13]   Interview with Joan Bakewell – BBC Television – 1966 – last shown in 2004 as part of BBC4's 1960's season.

[14]   Ibid

[15]   Picturegoer Magazine – April 19th 1952

[16]   Author interview with Roger Upton – 2005

[17]   Author interview with Stephen Frank – Birichen Moor – 2007

[18]   British Falconers Club Archive

[19]   Obituary, The Independent, September 25th 2000

[20]   Glasier, Phillip 'As The Falcon Her Bells' (Futura – 1977), p130

[21]   Ibid

[22]   Ibid

[23]   Ibid

[24]   Ibid

[25]   Picture Post, February 21st 1953

[26]   Glasier, Phillip 'As The Falcon Her Bells' (Futura – 1977), p131

[27]   Ibid, p132

[28]   Ibid, 135

[29]   Obituary, The Independent, September 25th 2000

[30]   Source unknown

[31]   Sunday Times, date unknown

[32]   Pettigrew, Terence 'British Character Actors' (Rowman & Littlefield – 1982), p176

[33]   Author interview with Martin Leslie – Isle of Skye – 2007

[34]   Ibid

[35]   Ibid

[36]   Ibid

[37]   Ibid

[38]   Ibid

CHAPTER 13:
DOCTOR IN THE HOUSE

In its first year of release, *Doctor in the House* (1954), the screen adaptation of Richard Gordon's comedy novel about the trials and tribulations of medical students, had attracted half the ticket-buying public in Britain and elevated Dirk Bogarde from just another romantic lead to a star overnight. But it was James Robertson Justice who, despite being on-screen for barely a third of the total running time, managed to encapsulate the character of Sir Lancelot Spratt to such an extent that it led to him becoming a permanent fixture in the film's six sequels. Yet incredibly the role that is forever linked to Justice might never have been his in the first place. The original choice for the crotchety medical ogre was Robert Morley, but the price his agent demanded was so ridiculously over inflated that the producers went straight to their second choice, James Robertson Justice. "And we've been thanking our lucky stars ever since," said Betty Box (who sadly died in 1999). "It wasn't the first time, and by no means the last, that a second and even a third choice for a part has turned out to be a lucky break for a movie, and the casting of Justice certainly added a big plus to the film."[1]

Ironically, when the movie opened to unanimously favourable press reviews, one critic in praising Justice's performance said: "In future, Robert Morley had better look to his laurels." Another amusing piece of trivia is that, years later in a stage version of *Doctor in the House* the role of Sir Lancelot Spratt was played by a young struggling actor by the name of Harold Pinter; an odd piece of casting to be sure. Pinter later revealed that the role gave him time during a long provincial tour to start his career as one of Britain's leading dramatists.[2]

Such is the impression Justice made as Sir Lancelot Spratt on the movie going public, that today it is he, and not the film's star, Dirk Bogarde, who is most associated with the Doctor series. "Whoever says to me Sir Lancelot Spratt is recalling not the character I created in the novel *Doctor in the House*, but James Robertson Justice," says Richard Gordon. "His arrival in the movie as the great surgeon of St. Swithin's Hospital was magnificent. Sporting black jacket and pin-striped trousers, marching majestically up the wide front steps, Rolls-Royce at the foot, graciously greeting his flanking white-coated assistants with "Good morning, gentlemen," then tossing his hat and cane accurately to an expectant porter, and it wasn't far from the truth. Nor was his ward-round, drawing vast incisions in red pencil across the frightened patient's abdomen, reassuring him not to bother with all this medical talk, barking unexpected questions at the students." At one point he invites Kenneth More's student to inspect a patient. More moves in to touch the man's abdomen. Justice explodes. "Take that grubby fist away. The first rule of diagnosis gentlemen, eyes first and most, hands next and least, and tongue not at all – Look!"[3]

And then arrives the moment which has since passed into movie folklore and is perhaps the most famous comedy moment in British fifties cinema. Surrounded by a gaggle of students, Justice is laying down the law about the curious behaviour of human blood, and the scientifically approved term, bleeding-time, when he spots Dirk Bogarde daydreaming. "You – what's the bleeding-time?" he barks, whereupon Bogarde, jolted back to reality, snatches a guilty look at his watch and replies, "Ten past ten, sir." It's utterly priceless.

Gordon actually appears in a cameo role in *Doctor in the House* during the operating theatre scene, playing Sir Lancelot's anaesthetist, the author's former profession. "It seemed to me perfectly normal his complaining loudly about the instruments," says Gordon. "And interrupting his commentary on the operation with only a brief "Catch him, someone!" as Dirk fainted at the sight of blood. We shot the hospital scenes in University College, Bloomsbury. James had studied science there. This allowed him to correct everyone on science, which I soon found included medical science."[4]

Betty Box herself found Justice a totally engaging character, the phrase larger than life might have been coined for him. One night everyone went for a well-earned aperitif to Harry's Bar, a favourite showbiz hang out. As Betty recalls, "I was with James when an American tourist lady, hung about with cameras and pixie-hoods, approached us. 'Tell me,' she twanged at James. 'Aren't you the

Author Richard Gordon (far left) sits in on a discussion of his comedy, 'Doctor in the House', with director Ralph Thomas (second left), editor Gerald Thomas (third left) & producer Betty Box (second right) after viewing the days' rushes. The film and its sequels were to make JRJ a household name. – 1953

great Ernest Hemingway?' James drew himself up to his full six feet something and boomed at her in his unforgettable voice, 'Madam, I am not your Mr Hemingway. And for your information, let me tell you that I am ten years younger than he, and at least ten inches taller.'"[5]

It's Betty Box we have to thank for the existence of the *Doctor* films. At that time Betty was the only female producer under contract with J. Arthur Rank. In fact, until the early 1960s she was the only female producer in the movies. Gearing up for a train journey back to London from Cardiff, Betty's publicist handed her a book from the station bookstall and suggested it would amuse her on the long trek home. It was *Doctor in the House* by Richard Gordon. "It was fortunate for my fellow travellers that we were in a corridor train on my way back from Cardiff," Betty later recalled. "I was enjoying reading *Doctor in the House* so much I didn't realise, until I got to the last page and the train was pulling into London, that my laughter had almost emptied the carriage. I closed the book with regret. Already I was missing the loveable characters Richard Gordon had brought to life so vividly"[6]

Betty's film making instincts told her that *Doctor in the House* had just the right ingredients for a happy-go-lucky contemporary comedy – just the type of movie the public wanted. Richard Gordon was then working as an anaesthetist in Oxford and was flattered that Betty wanted to buy the film rights to his first novel. "I'm happy that you like it," he told the producer over lunch. "But I'm told it won't work as a film. Associated British Films bought an option, but they couldn't lick it, so they gave it up."[7]

Betty could understand why. The novel wouldn't be easy to turn into a script; it had no real storyline. It was mainly a string of anecdotes about the life of a group of medical students, and she and director Ralph Thomas, older brother of *Carry On* director Gerald (not to mention editor of *Doctor in the House*) and father of producer Jeremy (who has films like *The Last Emperor* to his credit, as well as an Oscar) worked with three writers before they got the screenplay into a satisfactory shape.

Much of the charm of *Doctor in the House* comes from the interplay between the students, and Betty Box and Ralph Thomas were smart enough to cast engaging actors in all the various roles and good actors rather than comedians. "We decided to cast the actors that we would have done if it was going to be a straight dramatic story about medicine,"[8] recalled Thomas. Both had already worked with Kenneth More and knew that he was ideal casting for Grimsdyke, the perennial student – the one who intended to delay becoming a fully-fledged medico for as long as his inheritance lasted out. Donald Sinden, already under contract to Rank, was right for the amorous, girl-crazy Benskin, and for the rugger-playing student Donald Houston was cast, a star since his juvenile lead role opposite Jean Simmons in *The Blue Lagoon*.

To Betty's astonishment she encountered strong opposition from Rank's executive producer Earl St John to her choice of Dirk Bogarde to play the lead role of Simon Sparrow. He doubted Bogarde's capacity for comedy but Betty persuaded him to give the young actor a chance to read the script. Betty had worked only briefly with Bogarde on *So Long at the Fair*, but knew he was a more versatile screen actor than he'd yet been able to prove and desperately wanted him for Simon Sparrow. It was a turning point in his career. "Betty and Ralph had seen me in a couple of plays and realised that I could play comedy," said Bogarde. "The studio believed I could only play spivs and cockneys, but Betty and Ralph put me in tweeds and let me speak in my own voice, and the rest was history"[9]

Days after offering Bogarde the part the phone rang at Betty's country home. It was the young actor. He liked the script very much and would like to play young Simon Sparrow. There was just one thing. Kenneth More's part seemed to him to have more screen time, so he felt Betty should give him at least one extra scene.

"We'll talk about it," said Betty. "I'm sure we can work it out."

Then Betty's other phone started ringing. It was Kenneth More. "What a lovely script," he said. "But Dirk's part is bigger. I'll do it if you'll give me another scene or two."[10]

Betty smiled and decided not to tell More of her previous phone call.

Kenneth More had already appeared in two films with Justice prior to *Doctor in the House*. "I am very fond of him," he once told Betty. "He is a mountain of a man, the image of Henry VIII, with a fiercely glowing beard and twinkling blue eyes. Having been in his time a gold-miner, lumberjack, fruit farmer, insurance salesman, photographer, news agency reporter, ship's steward, schoolmaster and an ice rink manager, he reckons to know quite a bit about life. At lunch one day in the studio canteen, while waiting for James to arrive, several of us decided on a leg-pull. 'I'll pretend' said one of the chaps at the table, 'that my brother is a missionary in China and has just written to say that he's found a type of butterfly that has never been seen before. It's got blue spots on a pink background with yellow diagonal stripes. I bet you, though, James has heard of it!' When James joined us that's exactly what happened. At the mention of this phoney conversation of the butterfly, he didn't bat an eyelid. 'Oh, that's a very old species,' he said off-handedly. 'A relative of mine used to catch them in Tibet.'"[11]

The friend at my elbow whispered, "You can get away with murder if you play leading parts in films!"

Although Justice was an extremely popular member of the cast, not all of his colleagues held him in such high regard as the likes of More and Box. Donald Sinden worked with Justice several times over his long and distinguished career but they never really hit it off. "I'm afraid that we didn't really have very much in common" recalls Sinden. "James was a very gruff character and was always going on about country pursuits and the like. Not really my cup of tea at all. I tried several times to strike up conversations with him but always seemed to draw a blank. We were chalk and cheese really, and in the end didn't really converse at all."

Doctor in the House is full of delightful little cameo performances too. Shirley Eaton is delightful as a buxom landlady's daughter coming on strongly to a very convincingly uncomfortable Bogarde, and Kay Kendall is at her effervescent best as an upmarket Mayfair girl who catches Bogarde's eye. There was also a wonderful sequence featuring the comedian Tommy Cooper, doing his 'sawing the lady in half act,' which ended with mock disaster and Tommy's favourite cry, "Is there a doctor in the house?" Unfortunately this had to go. The film was over length and it was one of the few scenes that could be cut without losing continuity. What a shame!

As well as playing a cameo Richard Gordon was the film's medical advisor. It was his first experience of making movies and later described the director as, "the referee between artistes and technicians, shouting 'Action' and 'Cut' instead of blowing a whistle, his various assistants acting like linesmen." The film editor, he said, stands waiting, "like the pathologist in the operating theatre, knowing he'll soon have the film in his private mortuary for an entertaining post mortem." He was also complimentary of the sets, revealing that the film's operating theatre was so realistic that he automatically reached for his surgical mask each time he stepped on the set. "Even the actors playing patients, once in pyjamas and into bed, take on a mildly sickly appearance," he said.[12]

One of the film's highlights involved a students' rag and the kidnapping of St Swithin's Rugby team mascot, Gilbert, a huge, stuffed gorilla. Bags of flour and soot were liberally chucked around and there were fiendish cries as Bogarde and Co engaged in fierce hand-to-hand combat, faces streaked with black and white, and soda syphons squirting madly. The fracas in one of London's quiet, usually sedate, residential squares had to be seen to be believed. Crowds of onlookers were enjoying the chaos and laughing as Kenneth More, dressed as a nurse and wearing a blonde wig, rushed the gorilla on a stretcher into a waiting ambulance. Even the extras really let themselves go, three ending up in casualty; one with a broken arm, one with a gashed leg and another was a suspected concussion case.

A watching journalist reported: "Miss Box's battalion of stars staged a students' rag and before it finished, a £6,000 limousine was concertinaed by a furniture van; and an errand boy on a bike, badly knocked about, was retrieved from a window at the rear of a baker's van. Not one of Betty Box's embryo medicos proved very professional at first-aid treatment."[13]

After about half an hour of various hi-jinks, Sir Lancelot Spratt in his chauffeured Rolls enters and the film suddenly steps up several gears. Even in scenes where Justice is surgically masked and gowned, the sight of his beard and three-piece suit makes him instantly recognisable; his stentorian tones barking orders through his mask to all and sundry.

His bark, however, is proved to be more than his bite, when the students clash with a rival college and end up in front of a magistrate. Sparrow and his chums face stiff fines, too much for a quartet of penniless medical students to pay. The situation appears hopeless, until Justice's large, bearded, snuff-taking guardian angel steps in.

Richard Kneller, JRJ and Geoffrey Keen decide the fate of Messr's Sinden, Houston, More & Bogarde in the original and best Doctor film, 'Doctor in the House', 1954

To his friends and colleagues, Justice more often than not played himself on screen. He was an actor that didn't need to inhabit or subsume himself into a part as he tended to physically resemble the role he was given and played along with his own personality. But how much of that was true? "I would like to suggest that if one behaves absolutely as one does in private as one does on the screen it would come out as being far too vague," he once said. "In other words there must be a conscious effort to under-play a part. Even if you are playing it as yourself."[14] So in reality Justice was, if anything, under-playing his personality on screen.

But certainly the role of Sir Lancelot Spratt and James Robertson Justice was a match made in heaven. "It was a larger-than-life character that he barely had to bother to act, requiring little effort," so says one of his girlfriends, Molly Parkin. "For Sir Lancelot was James Robertson Justice."[15]

Far from merely drawing on his larger than life persona, Sir Lancelot was also based on a real person, a fellow ornithologist and surgeon that Justice knew very well. "He had a wonderful team in the operating theatre where he was very successful and they were all quite used to him. But he had a habit of using the most terrible language whilst operating. His team of course knew it was quite normal and everybody knew not to take offence. I know a lot of people will remember him when I use the word SNORKER. I won't mention his real name, but the name SNORKER will bring back memories to an awful lot of people."[16]

When it came time to release *Doctor in the House*, Rank bosses were still convinced that any film about hospitals spelt box-office poison, and were far from confident about its chances. Terrified of the medical plot, the studio publicity department even made the cast wear sports jackets instead of white coats in early press photographs. Worse, the sales force wanted to change the title to *Campus Capers*. "No film about doctors and hospitals has ever been successful," they announced to Betty and Thomas, "and we feel this title is more in key with the sort of movie you've made." They produced a poster with a group of young, American-type students sitting on the grass under a blossoming tree, eating apples and studying anonymous-looking books. "I almost vomited then and there," said Betty, who battled to keep her original title – and won.[17]

No one knew they had a hit on their hands until the producers attended a sneak preview of the film at a cinema in Edgware Road. The audience were cordial from the start, but the moment Justice barked at an inattentive Simon Sparrow, 'You, what's the bleeding time?' and received the reply, 'Ten past ten, Sir' the laugh was so enormous it drowned out the next scene and everyone knew they were on to something very big. When the film went on release three weeks later, it was greeted with critical rapture. But it was Justice who took the lion's share of praise. "Wonderful virtuoso appearance" said the Sunday Chronicle. Justice, "Storms through the film with such vitality" wrote the esteemed critic C. A. Lejeune.[18]

In its first year, an unprecedented 17 million tickets were sold, making *Doctor in the House* the most popular film of 1954 in the UK. Betty Box was overjoyed, though her fellow producer William MacQuitty calculated that there were 34 million people of cinema-going age in the country, so "why didn't the other 17 million go?"[19]

It's difficult to pinpoint exactly why *Doctor in the House* took off the way it did. One of the attractions to a post-war audience was the mild innuendo and the cocking a snook at authority, in this case stuffy doctors and the medical establishment. People had always held medicine in great awe, but in this film audiences could identify with the amusing situations on show, after all most people have been in hospital at one time or another. Although mild by today's standards, the first *Doctor* film was groundbreaking for the time and may have had an influence on another British comedy series that would rear its head four years later, the *Carry Ons*.

1   Author interview with Betty E Box – Pinewood Studios – July 1994

2   Box, Betty E.*'Lifting The Lid'* – The Book Guild (2000)

3   Letters to author from Richard Gordon – 2005

4   Ibid

5   Box, Betty E.*'Lifting The Lid'* – The Book Guild (2000)

6   Ibid

7   Ibid

8   Interview with Ralph Thomas, Classic Images, March 1996

9   Author interview with Betty E Box – Pinewood Studios – July 1994

10 Box, Betty E.*'Lifting The Lid'* – The Book Guild (2000)

11 Author interview with Betty E Box – Pinewood Studios – July 1994

12 Letters to author from Richard Gordon – 2005

13 Box, Betty E.*'Lifting The Lid'* – The Book Guild (2000)

14 Source unknown

15 Parkin, Molly *'Moll: Making of Molly Parkin'* (Gollancz – 1994)

16 Interview with Joan Bakewell – BBC Television – 1966 – last shown in 2004 as part of BBC4's 1960's season.

17 Box, Betty E.*'Lifting The Lid'* – The Book Guild (2000)

18 Ibid

19 Ibid

JRJ in the early 1950's, sporting the 'Robertson Clan' badge, Bracken, which bears the clan motto, Virtutis Gloria Merces – Glory is the reward of valour.

CHAPTER 14:
SPINNINGDALE

In 1954, with the money earned from his movie successes, Justice purchased a house called 'Spinningdale', situated just outside the village of Spinningdale on the Dornoch Firth in the north east of Scotland. This would become his main residence until he was forced to sell it in 1970. It was a large, rather secluded, single storied building built in the twenties by a colourful local character, Mr Chance. Today the house is known to the locals simply as 'The Bungalow'.

Justice loved the place; here he could enjoy fly-fishing, ornithology and falconry, renting the nearby Birichen Moor to exercise his birds. Above all he could enjoy in his passion for nature. He once wrote: "There are certain events during the course of the country year which are absolutely necessary to me if my life is to be as full as I like to flatter myself it should be. Such as the sight of a falcon stooping down the winter sky or a skein of geese flighting in from one of the great estuaries to their feeding grounds. A summer without hearing a good nightingale is hopelessly incomplete."[1]

Justice's passion for geese was well known amongst his friends. In the April 1952 edition of *Country Fair Magazine* he wrote, "When I lived in Galloway I saw badgers, otters, peregrines, merlins and harriers. But it is always to the geese that my memory turns." Indeed, Justice's favourite tie (which features regularly on the photographs herein) features a Peter Scott design depicting geese in flight.

Whilst at Spinningdale, Justice received a gift from Peter Scott in the shape of several pairs of Greylag and Barnacle geese. When they arrived Justice had a pond dug in a small field at the bottom of his garden, just beside the sea. After having their wings pinioned (or clipped) he set about getting the geese settled in the hope that they would breed, with the offspring eventually joining the seasonal migration. Some may indeed have migrated but many stayed, with only the Greylags breeding successfully. In fact they have been trying the patience of the local farmers ever since!

Justice assisted the booming population with regular feeding and they bred all over the place. Several families nested in the woods situated above the house, which meant that in order for them to reach the water they had to cross the busy A9. In an effort to prevent accidents happening Justice erected a sign on the side of the road reading "Caution – Young Geese Crossing!"

It gave Justice and his guests great pleasure to watch the geese flying over the house at rooftop height and then hearing them 'Whiffle' as they dropped down onto the pond and into the sea. That said, they could make a real mess if they happened to land a little short of the water. In order to prevent this happening, Justice would often order guests out to 'shoo' them on before they could set about destroying the garden.

Apart from birds, Justice's favourite things were hawk moths and orchids. He always said that if he had his time over again he would have become the world's expert on both.

As a child, Carol Davies lived across the Dornoch Firth from Justice's house, in a cottage, having moved up with her parents, brother and sister from Chester around the same time. Her father had got a job as the River Superintendent for the Kyle of Sutherland River Authority, supervising over 200 miles of river. "A few days after we arrived," Carol recalls, "there was a knock at the bungalow door and standing there was James Robertson Justice. I remember my sister and I being absolutely terrified. Standing there was this enormous man who literally filled the entire doorframe. Imposing wasn't the word. What I remember most though was the fact that he had a red spotted hanky in his top pocket and the most wonderful twinkly eyes! He also had with him a Black Pointer called Friday who we ended up looking after when he was away filming."[2]

Carol's childhood is filled with delightful memories of Justice, when she used to go to his home and sit on the floor on a huge soft white carpet that he had. "For some reason he absolutely adored me, much more than my brother and sister, and constantly asked my mother and father if he could adopt me – he used to say 'Let me have her, I can give her a wonderful upbringing' and believe it or not he was deadly serious. I used to plead with my parents to let me go because I'd be able to have a horse (that was my dream at the time but my parents couldn't afford one). Needless to say I never got to go. I also remember his car and one day he actually came and picked me up from school at Larachan in it. It was unbelievable. Can you imagine getting picked up from school by James Robertson Justice in a big posh car! I was the envy of the school for weeks."[3]

Carol's father and Justice shared an interest in wildlife and in particular, falcons. "They spent hours together on the moors," recalls Carol "and my Father enjoyed every minute".[4] An occasional guest on these expeditions was Prince Philip, who made several visits to Spinningdale in the late 1950's and early 1960's.

Justice was one of the few people to have his own electricity supply, thanks to a generator working on the old mill apparatus that he'd resurrected which used to feed the spinning mill that gave Spinningdale its name. Guests would be quite happy sitting having supper, or eventually when Justice had acquired a television, watching a programme, when all of a sudden the picture would go down or the lights started going dim. As soon as that happened, the guests had already been instructed on what to do. They just rose from wherever they were sitting and ran like hell to the pit into which the water came. Inside there were these great big cast-iron grids going down into the pit and the guest had to grab a big wire-headed rake and rake all the leaves off that had built-up on them to get the electricity back on.

Spinningdale would open its doors to guests regularly, but very few from the film world were ever invited. Betty Box was perhaps one of the few film colleagues of Justice that got an invite. "The gardens there were lovingly nurtured by James," she recalled. "He went every year to Holland to select his bulbs and whenever he visited my house he left with boxes of cuttings of our very special azaleas and rhododendrons."[5]

Other guests included the novelist Eric Linklater and would-be falconry experts like Roger Upton and Stephen Frank. There was also another chap whose father was a Presbyterian minister. He had lived a relatively sheltered life and Justice recognised this and promptly set-about personally seeing to it that a very beautiful, lovely young woman made sure he was much more worldly wise by the time he left. He was always exceptionally grateful to him for that![6]

Then there was Captain Mike Fell, who had been posted-up as the Commanding Officer at Lossiemouth, the Royal Naval Air Station. He used to come across to Spinningdale for drinks and dinner. Repaying the hospitality Justice would be asked across to see him and told to bring whomever he wished. One day Justice drove over to visit Fell, who had a very beautiful lady staying with him. Redheaded, wonderful figure, her name was Rusty, and she was a tremendous character. Fell had a great sense of humour and had also invited his naval chaplain to lunch because he knew that he was the type of man who would more than happily take Justice on, atheist or agnostic or whatever he claimed to be. Fell knew that Justice had an extensive knowledge of the Bible and also knew that his chaplain was even more skilled in this respect. Fell briefed the chaplain and so it wasn't long until, over the lunch-table, this man of God quietly floated a quotation from the Bible across the conversation to have Justice immediately float another one back. It was like ping-pong, they swapped quotations back and forth as suitable to the moment in the conversation. And the two men continued this exchange by postcard for several years afterwards.[7]

After lunch Justice took off to see his old friend, the Laird of Pitgaveny. Captain Fell, his wife, and Rusty went too. The old Laird had a good eye for the ladies, although he was well into his eighties at that time, and as soon as Rusty walked across the threshold his eyes never left her. As she walked into the sitting room the Laird walked all round her, looking at her quite exceptional figure. Rusty had been warned that something like this might happen, and was chuckling away, taking him on. "Man, man…" the Laird said, "I'd surely like to see that with no clothes on." Without a pause Rusty dropped her skirt and stepped out of it and stood there in her panties. The old gentleman, for the only time in his life that anyone could remember, was totally lost for words. His moustache was going up and down and his eyes were twinkling and everybody just roared with laughter. The old Laird always loved calling people's bluffs, and he called hers and Rusty called his.[8]

Another regular visitor at Spinningdale was Martin Leslie. After *Rob Roy* Leslie had heard hide nor hare of Justice, and wasn't much surprised. "Then a year later I was going to the Northern Meeting (a Highland Ball) one night in Inverness. I was just stepping over the threshold of the Northern Meeting rooms when somebody hit me between the shoulder blades and propelled me forward practically onto my knees. I couldn't think who could possibly have done this to me and I spun-round and there was this enormous, bearded presence asking me where I'd been. He'd certainly had a dram, he was on cracking form and he said: "Now, write down your telephone number on my programme and we will be in touch. I now live in Spinningdale, it's a lovely place. You'll come and see me." But again, I never expected to hear anything. And was therefore, fully amazed when, about a fortnight later, he rang up and said, 'Right, what are you doing next weekend? Come up' which was the first time I went up to Spinningdale. It was a lovely place."[9]

JRJ outside his new home, Spinningdale, where he was to spend many of his happiest years. (Stephen Frank)

At Spinningdale Leslie met Phillip Glasier, "who was probably the only professional falconer at the time. We'd go up to the hill and I began to learn a little bit about falcons and how they work. Phillip Glasier looked like a falcon and was brilliant with them. He clearly got on very well with James and they really enjoyed going to the hill together.[10]

When Martin Leslie was studying to become a chartered land agent, Justice suggested that he spend his $2^1/_2$ weeks leave from work to prepare for exams in the "peace and quiet" of Spinningdale. "James was of the opinion that classical music – played very loudly – was necessary background for studying and moved a loud speaker into the room he'd put aside for me. In addition, coffee and alcoholic beverages were served regularly. There must have been something in it as both exams were passed first time. Something never before experienced in my case!"

He never forgot one July, though, the year after his visits began, when Justice phoned him one afternoon asking for a favour. Could he go and collect, from Inverness, a four year-old English pointer bitch called Robina who'd been given to him by Lord Rank? The famous film tycoon and businessman was handing her over because she was no use for shooting; she was gun-shy, but thought she'd be fine for falconry. "She'll be coming up in a crate," said Justice on the phone, "and if you'll kindly post the crate back, keep a note of any expense and I'll reimburse you. I won't be up for another 10 days or something so if you can keep her for me." Leslie already owned a black Labrador and his family had an old Spaniel so one more dog wasn't going to make that much difference. "And, like a lamb to the slaughter, I went and collected the most beautiful English Pointer I probably have ever seen. She came with leads and with whistles. All were labelled with beautiful, copper-plate handwriting. You blew this one and the dog came back to you. You blew that one and at the end of her run, she would turn and cast at the other side. You blew the third one and she would stop."[11]

Leslie tested the dog out one day in a field and found to his astonishment that she did everything that the whistles commanded her to do and rang Justice in an excited mood. "You've got a fantastic dog. She's so biddable; she's as soft as butter." Then the problems started. Leslie had to go off somewhere and left the dog in his room at his parent's house. On his return he got a frosty reception. Robina had yelled the place down till she was hoarse and had completely destroyed his bedroom door trying to get out. Not surprisingly, Leslie couldn't wait to get her back up to Spinningdale and to Justice. "I demonstrated her upon the lawn," recalls Leslie, "and James was duly impressed. We took her to the hill the next day, a beautiful day. Took her up to Birichen Moor and set her off, running. Well, she went, and she went, and I blew the 'turn' whistle and she paid no attention. I blew the 'drop' whistle and she paid no attention. I blew the 'come back to me' whistle and she paid no attention. We watched her disappear into the distance. She put grouse up in every direction and she paid no heed to anything. In the fullness of time, about ten minutes later, she turned-round and came back. And I stood in her way and held my hand up and blew all the whistles, one after the other, and she swerved round me and ran another half-mile in the other direction. So we all sat down in the sunshine. I remember old James sat on this rock and wasn't the least put-out. He was just having a quiet chuckle, and said that he'd have a word or two with Lord Rank next time he saw him. Eventually Robina came back and threw herself down beside us, a yard and a half of tongue hanging-out, and basically indicated, 'I've had the most wonderful time!' She was completely, and utterly, useless. She was hopeless because she was also totally gun shy. If you went to the gunroom in Spinningdale she was up the curtains, she was under the furniture, she was absolutely, mortally terrified."[12]

Realising that the dog would be useless for practical purposes, Justice decided instead to try her out for breeding as her looks and pedigree were so good. "Over the next year or so he tried her with every aristocratic Pointer in the north of Scotland," says Leslie. "Robina damn-near killed the lot of them. She would have nothing to do on the amorous front." Justice had all but given up on Robina when he went to lunch with Colin Campbell, up above Ardgay. Campbell and his wife Sue were regular visitors at Spinningdale. "Sue was a really nice, very beautiful woman," says Leslie. "And James, I think, would dearly loved to have seduced her. But because he liked Colin very much it would have been a total disaster, so he didn't actually try. He was seen-off when he got too familiar anyway; she was well up to his behaviour."[13]

Campbell had a German Pointer dog, and he spotted Robina in the back of Justice's car when he arrived and said: "Bring her into lunch, we all know Robina."

"No, no, no," insisted Justice. "She's on heat and I don't want any more vets bills!"

Campbell just laughed: "No, just let her out. If she's seen-off all the aristocratic Pointers in the north she's just been waiting for the continental touch!"

Justice remained anxious. "Well, she'll fix your fellow as well! And the vet's bill's are expensive."[14]

But Campbell was adamant so Justice finally relented. "On your own head be it," he said, but no sooner had he opened the back door of the car than the two dogs were firmly joined in the matrimonial grip. And, 63 days later, Robina gave birth to four beautiful, half-English, half-German Pointer puppies.

As Leslie recalls, one went to Toby Bromley for his son, while another went to the owner of the Shandwick Inn, between Tain and Invergordon, and became known as the finest rough-shooting man's dog in the north-east of Scotland. Her reputation was so great that she was stolen when she was about five and a half. "And about eight months later she was found dead on the railway," recalls Leslie. "She must have escaped from whoever stole her, and she was making her way home, up the railway, and she was only half a mile away. And her toenails were worn right down to the quick. And she was as lean as can be. It was an absolute tragedy."[15]

Justice himself kept a pup and called her, in Gaelic, 'Sorach', or 'Primrose'. When she was six months old Justice again rang Leslie asking for a favour. His mother was currently living at Spinningdale, and it was not going well – the arrangement did not last. He'd brought her up from Hampshire because he was worried about her. Cathy Martin, Justice's lovely West Highland housekeeper, was looking after her. Problems began when the pup was wont to go out and dig-up the garden, which annoyed Mrs. Justice, who rang the bell for the gardener. When Cathy came she informed Mrs. Justice that the gardener only came for about four hours a week when he felt like it. So it was some time, perhaps days, before the man arrived and he was sent for and promptly told to go and beat the dog. Naturally the gardener did not want to carry out such an order. "The dog doesn't know what it's done wrong," he said. But Mrs. Justice was adamant. "If you know what's good for you," she told him. "And you want to keep your job; you'll go and sort it out."[16]

The little dog's unhappiness continued and it eventually went to live in the Rhododendron bushes. Finally Justice called Leslie from where he was filming to see if he could collect her and take her back with him saying: "If you can't make anything of her with your black Labrador you must take her to the vet and have her put-down, and I'll pay the bill." Luckily that was the beginning of a wonderful relationship with Sorach and often Leslie would bring her down to Spinningdale when Justice was at home and she became a very good falconers' dog. "She was brilliant but she was gun-shy, like her mother, and yet she'd never seen a gun; didn't know what it was for. She just got terribly traumatised if she saw a gun. Maybe her mother told her something. Anyway, she lived happily at Spinningdale for the rest of her days."[17]

"Sorach's mother, Robina also had a very annoying ability," remembers Leslie. "She could find the most dreadfully rotten carrion, roll in it and then come home, well 'scented' with great pride! This despite the fact that she would then have to be hosed down before going into the cold kennel until she smelled pure enough to come back into the house. Robina loved the warmth, comfort and company of being a very spoilt house dog!

"When I was at Spinningdale studying for exams at a time of deep snow, the local farmer decided to empty his 'midden' and put it out onto the field nearby in three foot high heaps, ready for spreading when the snow was gone. A midden is a dung heap and in the old days could contain all manner of agricultural waste, occasionally including long-dead calves!

"Robina and Sorach came back covered in muck and smelling of something awful. I heard Cathy's voice raised in anger, went to see what was wrong, and met James coming in from the kennel who told me to come and help him out. I washed the dogs down, scrubbed them with 'Lifebuoy' soap, dried them off and put them into the kennel, which had a good straw bed. Eventually, unbeknownst to me, James relented and let them back in to the sitting room by the fire where he was. About an hour later I suddenly heard James yell, 'Watch out! Shut the door!' Too late, the dogs got out of the sitting room, sprinted down the passage to the back door, through Cathy and the postman's legs and were gone. I ran after them, tracking them easily in the snow which continued to fall and could see them sliding down a particular heap, on their backs, wriggling to make sure they got covered in the jellified, malodorous remains of a very long-dead calf. This time both dogs remained in the kennel overnight but the smell was with us for days!"

Eventually Justice discovered why Robina was gun-shy and phoned Leslie: "You know the little things you thought were sebaceous cysts at the back of her ear that kept appearing? I was sitting, fondling her ear and one of these things was there and I was just working my thumbnail on it and it popped-out in my hand. It was a piece of six-shot." After that he collected about 16 bits of six-shot and reckoned she'd probably been blasted in the backside for not obeying whistles and the shot had migrated up to the back of her ears. "It solved the problem as to why she was gun-shy," says Leslie, "and probably why she told her daughter not to have anything to do with guns either. But she was a much-loved house-dog."[18]

By the early fifties Justice's mother had been living in Nether Wallop in Hampshire, residing in a beautiful rambling house called Pyles Farm. A few hundred yards up the road was a ten-year-old boy called Brian Rivas, who along with a friend would visit the elderly Mrs. Justice. "She must have been about 70 years old, or at the very least in her late sixties and was the loveliest and kindest of ladies," recalls Rivas. "She always made the two of us most welcome and we had tremendous fun when she had bulldozers and other machinery in to do some major landscaping on her large garden. More than anything I recall the warmth of her smile and her friendly and welcoming manner to us boys. She was a very gentle and kind person and you immediately felt at home with her."[19]

It was on one of Rivas' visits that Justice himself rolled up in a gull-wing Mercedes 300SL, "and announced to us in that unforgettable voice that he had been looking for a certain butterfly in the New Forest but 'couldn't find the damned thing.' We were a little in awe of him."[20]

A frequent visitor to Mrs Justice was 'Chunky' Horne, a test pilot for Supermarine at nearby Chilbolton who was doing a lot of flying on prototypes of the Swift jet fighter. "Chunky was one of my childhood heroes," says Rivas. "So it was very exciting to meet him. He was very good looking and a most charming man who always took the time to have a chat with us. Chunky could be a bit of madman in the air, but ironically it was when he was a passenger in an Austin Healey that he suffered terrible injuries in a road accident and was never really the same again."[21]

When Rivas was preparing for his first day at public school, something he wasn't looking forward to, Mrs. Justice made an iced sponge cake for him to take to classes. "To this day I recall the sight, taste and texture of that cake. A few weeks later my parents had moved to Ringwood and I never saw Mrs. Justice again, but she was a lady I will never forget and I will always remember with fondness the happy times I had as a child at her home."[22]

In the late 1960s Brian Rivas was at a filling station in Stockbridge when who should pull up at the pumps but James Robertson Justice himself. "I went up to him and explained that I used to know his mother well and asked how she was. 'Dead,' he replied. Just that, nothing more – and the way he said it didn't exactly encourage further questioning, so I just muttered that I was very sorry to hear that. But I heard later, although I know nothing of the circumstances; that she died of malnutrition. I was shocked and upset to hear that this beautiful lady had come to what sounded like a very sad and undeserved end."[23]

Spinningdale was a place where Justice could give free rein to his eccentricities. He liked nothing better, for example, than to wake people up by playing Mozart's Horn Concerto on a length of garden hose, which he kept expressly for the purpose, and which he wrapped-round himself. This he would do by introducing the end of the hose through the bedroom door and then blasting merrily away. "It shocked quite a number of people into wakefulness," recalls Martin Leslie. "And gave me a lot of fun when I knew he was going to do it. He also played the piano very well. Also he was the only person I ever met who played Mozart on the bagpipes."[24]

Practical jokes were also encouraged. One of Justice's favourites was when he had guests staying overnight. The rooms upstairs in the loft were all timber-walled and there was a secret way of getting in behind them. When some young ladies were staying Leslie was encouraged to go up there and hammer nails into the support walls and hang cowbells on them. These were worked by strings which came down the back of the wall and into the room where Justice kept his gramophone. So when these unfortunate young women went to bed, Justice could pull on these strings and all hell was let-loose upstairs because they couldn't find from where the hellish noise was coming.

Justice's housekeeper Cathy had no choice but to put-up with Justice's eccentricities, where many others wouldn't have, and as a result they got-on like a house on fire. She used to rib him about his womanising and other matters and also entered into all the practical jokes which were played upon people as Leslie fondly recalls: "One evening the house was full of people so I had to sleep in the room with the bells and I said, 'I hope there are going to be no damn bells rung' and Justice said, 'no, no....there'll be no bells rung.' Well, the person who rang the bells was Cathy. I managed to get into this secret place and along the back of the wall and grabbed the bell off the hook. Afterwards I was quite determined that I was going to get Cathy. I shot out of the room and grabbed the door handle, and it was covered in treacle, which Cathy had put there! I rushed to the stair, grabbed the newell post, and she'd covered that with treacle as well. Down the stairs, she'd locked herself in her sitting-room and was crying with mirth. 'I got you that time!' she said, absolutely weeping the words. I camped on the doorstep but she wouldn't come out. I was peeled-off in the end and James said, 'you'll have to let her be, because otherwise we'll not get fed!' But that was the sort of thing that could go on at Spinningdale."[25]

When Cathy married George Fraser, who worked for the local council and lived in Ardgay, the ceremony took place at Spinningdale and the celebrations were memorable to say the least. Cathy's relatives came over from Skye, including grandmothers and her brother, who was a merchant naval sea captain. "Now, stag-nights can be difficult," says Leslie. "And there are awful Highland traditions which involve doing terrible things to the bridegroom. George was nervous, to put it mildly." Fearing what was to be done with him, George fled from the social gathering the night before the wedding. "I think we'd better go and find him," said the merchant navy Captain, in a wonderful West Highland voice. So Leslie, the captain and another guest went looking for the groom. In the end he was found hiding in a rhododendron bush on the drive at Spinningdale. The naval captain reached in and plucked out a furious George who kicked out and yelled at the top of his voice, but the Captain held him in a bear-grip and crooned into his ear, "we mean you no harm, no harm at all, but there are certain traditions that have to be upheld."[26]

The group went down to Justice's house and in front was a Bedford Dormobile which Justice used for fetching people from the station and such like. Everyone got in and the captain produced a bottle of whisky out of one pocket and a footed glass out of another. He then knocked the foot off the glass, saying "Ach – we will not be wanting to put it down again tonight!"

"George was between me and this other man who had a firm grip of him so that he couldn't bolt," recalls Leslie. "The captain said: "Ach well, now we can get started. Drink your health George." We emptied the whole bottle of whisky in about an hour. George must have had most of it and wasn't in the best of trim when we took him back to his digs and tucked him up in bed. The following morning, his wedding day, we thought we'd better go and make sure he was alright. He wasn't brilliant but we got him sobered-up with lots of black coffee and a walk in the fresh air."[27]

Even at the wedding, Spinningdale's reputation for practical-joking had continued. "Birdseed was a very favourite thing to put in people's luggage," recalls Leslie. "And then when ladies got home and took out their nightie, or whatever, there was birdseed everywhere. So Cathy's case had been well doctored. George, very wisely, had locked his, we couldn't get into it. The couple had hired this car and a very nice man as driver and we had decided that in order to give them the right send-off we would have one last kiss with Cathy. When she got in the car we asked her to wind-down the window. She was very nervous but we said: 'Come-on Cathy, you've got to do this.' She was afraid of what might happen. When she opened the window we let-go two pigeons that we'd caught with fishing-nets in the dark the previous night and she was yelling blue-murder. The poor man who was the chauffeur was haring up the drive in this car with the two pigeons flying-loose in it. And to our absolute horror the car just made it round the bend of the drive when we heard this crash. We ran up the drive and the poor man....the pigeons had been flying-around him and he'd lost his vision for a minute and he'd run-into a tree. He'd broken a head-light and bent the front of the car a bit, all of which James paid for at the end of the day, so he wasn't enthusiastic as the couple were driven out onto the road to start their married life together! But it was the start of some night."[28]

The wedding itself took place in the drawing-room at Spinningdale and at the party later everybody was determined to have a great time. But Justice faced a problem, the women sat on one side, the men sat on the other, and he'd prepared some music on his gramophone to get people up and dancing. The grandmothers from Skye were not in a party mood and were casting a dampener on the proceedings. "Look, somehow or other we have got to get those two groups underway. If the Grandmothers refuse champagne then try and offer them Ginger Ale, and hope that they say yes. Until we get them to join in nothing will happen."

Leslie and two students went across to the stony-faced grandmothers and said, "Ladies, would you like a dram or perhaps you'd like to try something soft – like ginger ale?"

They looked at each other and said: "We don't like ale, that's beer. We don't like ale."

"No, no," said Leslie. "This is a ginger drink. I'll get the bottle."

Bottles of Ginger Ale were produced. The two Grandmothers looked at the label and duly discussed the matter and said: "Oh ginger, well yes, we quite like a bit of ginger. Perhaps…yes, we'll try the ginger. That's very kind."

The students went back and James surreptitiously poured a shot of brandy into the bottom of the glasses before pouring in the ginger ale. The Grandmothers both took a little sip and one of them said: "Oh, that's, that's just fine! Oh well, it's got a lovely taste. Has it not got a lovely taste?" It was quaffed down rather rapidly and the party never looked back. They were all up on the floor, doing the Reels, everything.[29]

"The party continued for a long time," confirms Leslie. "James had paid for a piper to play as the married couple left. Later on I found the piper in the conservatory, absolutely gone. He could hardly speak and was more or less incapable of movement; it was quite disgraceful. James came along to see if he could help, but the man swore blind that he could get home and off he went through the field, but he never made it. He went to sleep in the field…..where he was found the next morning."[30]

The following day Leslie and the students began the awesome task of clearing up, despite the fact that they were suffering quite badly from a hangovers. To get on they all downed a 'Prairie Oyster,' which roughly is a raw egg in the bottom of a glass, a little white wine, a little cayenne pepper, a little brandy and Worcestershire sauce. Then you swirl it round and swallow the yolk whole. Justice was not feeling at all well and didn't really appear for a while and of course there was no Cathy to do anything. So Leslie and the two students set about clearing everything up. There were God knows how many left-over drinks in glasses and when Justice finally emerged he said: "We mustn't throw the drink away, it will be very good for cooking." He produced various large, empty whisky bottles and things and said: "Just put it in the bottles and put them in the cupboard. Cathy will sort it out when she gets back."

This Leslie and the students did. "We didn't know what we were putting into the bottles," Leslie recalls. "But we ended up with about five full bottles that we put into this cupboard in the kitchen. Then we decided that we needed a little peace and quiet.....and rest. It was a lovely sunny afternoon. We went up onto the roof; you could actually recline against one roof and let the sun beat-down upon you. We were relaxing up there when we heard the first explosion. We hurtled downstairs to find that one of the bottles into which we'd put this mixture had burst, and the stuff was running down the wall. A terrible mess! We had an awful time clearing it up. James, when eventually he came through....er....groaning, and saw the mess, and what we were doing, said: "You'd better get that sorted-out otherwise Mrs. Fraser, as now is, is not going to be at all pleased."[31]

[1]   Justice, James Robertson 'A Merry Year' – Country Fair Magazine, July 1955

[2]   Author interview with Carol Davies – 2006

[3]   Ibid

[4]   Ibid

[5]   Author interview with Betty E Box – Pinewood Studios – July 1994

[6-18] Author interview with Martin Leslie – Isle of Skye – 2007

[19-23] Correspondence to author – November 2006

[24-31] Author interview with Martin Leslie – Isle of Skye – 2007

Top Left: A sketch of JRJ drawn by Sir Peter Scott in 1948, the same year that he founded The Wildlife & Wetlands Trust, which JRJ was a founder member. The original still hangs in the home of Sir Peter's widow, Lady Philippa Scott. (Lady Philippa Scott) Top Right: JRJ and his favourite Peregrine Falcon 'Siubhalch' (which is gaelic for swift) on the moors close to his Hampshire home in 1953. Bottom: James' famed punt gun, Irish Tom being fired during a demonstration at the Holkham Country Fair in 1984 by Squadron Leader Mike Townsend. (Graham Downing)

Top Left: A still from 'The Sword & the Rose' as featured on a cover of Picture Post magazine in 1953. Top Right: With Brenda de Banzie in 'Doctor at Sea', 1955. Bottom: With Barbara Murray and Stanley Baker in 'Campbell's Kingdom', 1957

Top: Stanley Baxter, Jeremy Lloyd and Leslie Phillips welcome JRJ to his first leading role, as Sir Ernest Pease in the 1961 film 'Very Important Person'. Bottom: A German publicity still for 'Love on a Pillow' (1962) JRJ's second film with 'La Bardot' and first with director Roger Vadim.

Top Left: Outside Spinningdale in 1963. (Roderick Bromley) Top Right: JRJ and friends enjoying an afternoon at Pitcalzean House in Pitcalnie, Scotland. The then home of Eric and Marjorie Linklater. Shown Left to right: Phillip Glasier, complete with Goshawk, of course. Martin Leslie, who has contributed enormously to this book and kindly allowed us to use the photo, the then chaplain of Lossiemouth Naval base (and religious sparring partner to JRJ) whose name I'm afraid escapes us, the Laird of Pitgaveny's favourite redhead, Rusty, Mrs Mike Fell, Captain Mike Fell and lastly JRJ's mother, who was always known to the above as Ma Jus. Bottom: A rare screen kiss for JRJ, with Barbara Murray in 'Doctor in Distress', 1963

Top: JRJ and Toby Bromley, preparing a shoot for The Falcon Gentle in 1970 (Roderick Bromley)
Bottom: As Edward, Prince of Wales in the Terence Young film, 'Mayerling' – 1968

Above: A poster for 'Doctor in Clover', the sixth in the series but certainly not the best – 1966. Right: A bust of JRJ from his pre-beard days, in the garden at Spinningdale in 1970. It now sits proudly on top of Martin Leslie's fridge! (Martin Leslie)
Below: Spinningdale in 1970, shortly before James and Irina were forced to move out. (Martin Leslie)

Top Left: JRJ, Gordon Jolly, Irina and Stephen Frank near Spinningdale in the mid 1960's. (John Loft at The British Falconers Club). Top Right: James' pointer, Robina (facing the camera) and a few friends, on the sofa at Spinningdale – 1970 (Martin Leslie) Bottom: Fishing on the River Test during the making of Toby Bromley's nature film, 'The Chalk Stream Trout', 1974. This was, quite fittingly, JRJ's last ever appearance on film. (Roderick Bromley)

Top Left and Right: JRJ relaxing in the living room at Spinningdale – 1970 (Martin Leslie)
Bottom: James' final resting place on Birichin Moor, Scotland (James Hogg)

CHAPTER 15:
AT SEA IN HOLLYWOOD

Even before the phenomenal success at the British box office of *Doctor in the House*, the perceptive Betty Box had already optioned Richard Gordon's follow-up novel *Doctor at Sea*, based on the writer's observations and adventures as a ship's doctor – an assignment he took to give himself a break from hospital work while he wrote *Doctor in the House*.

The sequel, made in 1955, continued the already established *Doctor* formula, although this time the action takes place offshore, as Sparrow takes up a post as ship's doctor. Dirk Bogarde was more than happy to reprise his role as the young medic, but the impact of Justice's Sir Lancelot Spratt on audiences caused red faces at Rank Studios because the follow-up had made no provision for the character. The problem was overcome by casting Justice as the ship's captain and making the character indistinguishable from the bolshie head surgeon of St Swithin's.

Unlike the real Justice, Captain Hogg is an unashamed misogynist, who finds it a total anathema to have to carry women on board. "I don't approve of women, you understand," he says in the film. "They're unseamanlike and unnecessary." For the purposes of the plot, not one but two female passengers make their way on to his ship. The man-hungry Muriel Mallett, as played by the ever excellent Brenda de Banzi, spends most of her time pursuing the captain, but the crusty bachelor is deaf to her romantic overtures. "Steamship lines do like their Commodores to be married," she coos but old bristle face is having none of it. He is oblivious to any attempt to make him jealous – when Miss de Banzie enquires rather cheekily if she can borrow one of his dishier officers Justice growls, "Madam, as far as I'm concerned, you can keep him!"

Then there's Brigitte Bardot, the young French starlet, just 19 at the time, who plays Sparrow's love interest. Bardot, in her English-speaking debut and years away from becoming an international sex symbol, was a joy to work with, and before long had won the hearts of most of the unit. Her fractured English charmed everyone. Asked if she would go to a premiere by one of the actors, her face fell. "I'd be enchantée,' she said, "but sadly, I do not 'ave my nightdress wiz me."[1] Relatively unknown at the time, Bardot had been seen by Betty Box and Ralph Thomas in a few small French pictures. "She was very beautiful and ever such a talented actress," Thomas explained. "And you could tell straight away that she was something special."[2]

Justice struck up an unlikely rapport with Bardot, able to spend hours chatting in French with her. "James loved pretty girls,"[3] recalls Betty Box, "and on the occasions where we had continental actresses in the Doctor films he was always to be found chatting up either Bardot, or Mylene Demonngeot or Miss Austria or Budapest or whoever, in her own language."[4]

Although she was to become, in a few years' time, the World's No. 1 Sex Symbol, when told that she had a scene in which she'd have to appear nude in the shower in Bogarde's cabin, Brigitte wrinkled her nose, pouted and said, "We will 'ave to see how well Dirk and I get to know one another. I'm not sure I want to do eet." However, when the day dawned, a clutch of wardrobe and make-up ladies gathered around her carrying bath towels, kimonos, flesh-coloured bras and briefs – the usual paraphernalia demanded in those days by any British actress asked to show more than her cleavage. Brigitte took off her bathrobe and stood unselfconsciously in tiny briefs. "You can tell me, Ralph, when I goes in the shower, when I am to take off my knickers, OK?"[5] And off they came. No mucking about, and the scene was shot. Just to be on the safe side Thomas also shot the scene through a semi-transparent shower screen, and that was all they were allowed to use in the final print of the film. Bloody shame!

With interiors shot at Pinewood, location work took the cast and crew out to the vastly more palatial environs of the Mediterranean. Work took place on two real Greek liners, the Agamemnon, which was sailing from Italy to Egypt and Greece, and its sister ship, the Achilles, in dry dock at Piraeus in Greece, nicely refurbished and perfect for shooting the portside sequences. Justice didn't enjoy himself as much on the Agamemnon. Betty Box didn't discover until the second week of the voyage that Justice was having difficulty sleeping in his cabin because he was too bulky for the bunk. The only time he got into it

Top: JRJ as Captain Hogg in 'Doctor at Sea'. Seen here putting the fear of God in to Dirk Bogarde! Bottom: "I don't approve of women, they're unseamanlike and unnecessary". But that doesn't put off Brenda de Banzie, 'Doctor at Sea', 1955

he found he was all too firmly wedged, and took nearly an hour to extricate himself. "I didn't want to make a fuss," he said as Betty found him sleeping on the floor. "I'm quite happy here. I can't sink any lower."[6]

In the story, the ship has at one point to be abandoned and the passengers take to the lifeboats. The first lifeboat was to carry Bogarde, Bardot and Brenda de Banzie, as well as several other actors, and while everyone was busy in make up Ralph Thomas decided to have a trial run at lowering the lifeboat. Several crew members and a couple of electricians were put into the lifeboat; a big, bearded sailor sat in for Bardot, and the winching operation began. Everyone watched in horror as the metal chain on which the boat was being lowered snapped, and the boat upended and dangled precariously above the ocean. One Greek crew member was already overboard and the others hung desperately on to whatever they could grab until helping hands could haul them safely back on deck. The alarm was sounded, but the ship was at full speed and the unlucky seaman was rapidly disappearing from sight. The Greek captain turned his ship and headed back to the spot where the accident had happened.[7]

Luckily the Mediterranean Sea was behaving itself and was calm and flat and everyone heaved sighs of relief as a tiny dot in the far distance gradually grew larger and there was the crew member, apparently none the worse for his adventure. Hauled back on board he bowed charmingly and offered to do it all again, particularly when he received a special kiss from Bardot. She was no doubt thinking, as many were, that it could so easily have been herself catapulted into the water.

Justice looked very grand in his captain's uniform, particularly his summer whites, well-cut but voluminous white knee-length shorts, socks and shoes, white shirt and cap. Betty Box recalled that when the ship manoeuvred its way through the narrow Corinth Canal with a few inches to spare either side, "the women who were working in the fields which run down to the water's edge rushed, giggling, to stare at this splendid, bearded figure of a man on the bridge of the Agamemnon, his knees a rosy red in the winter breeze, his beard as immaculate as ever. I thought it a pity they weren't close enough to smell the spicy French eau de toilette he always used and which still reminds me of him now that he's no longer with us. He was a true original – a really lovely man."[8]

When the team arrived in Athens shooting continued aboard the Achilles. One of the film's most important sequences was a grand cocktail party aboard ship. Alas no matter how hard Betty Box scoured Athens she couldn't find anyone who looked remotely like the sophisticated glamourous crowd necessary for the scene to work. Betty had organised a small party for the evening – a get-together with the people who were allowing them to shoot in

Greece and, at the same time, an opportunity to meet the Greek press and publicise the movie. All the cast were present and Betty had asked the British Embassy to help select the appropriate local guests. "James Robertson Justice was invaluable with his endless knowledge of languages," said Betty. "I heard him speaking at least eight different languages during the evening and he was in great demand, as always."[9]

Sir Charles Peake, then the British Ambassador in Athens, was very sympathetic about the difficulty Betty was having trying to recruit people for the party scenes in the film and he and Lady Peake offered, not only to find a glamourous crowd from amongst their own friends and acquaintances, but also to come for the main filming themselves. True to their word they brought with them representatives of various foreign powers colourfully dressed in uniforms or national dress. It proved a memorable evening as the Greek waiters served the distinguished guests with pukka champagne instead of the cold tea or coloured water usually handed round for film party scenes.

Before the crew left Athens, Lady Peake invited the cast to the embassy for a farewell party, "where James Robertson Justice excelled himself with his inexhaustible repertoire of amusing stories,"[10] Betty recalled.

With on-screen temper tantrums resembling those of a gigantic, irate toddler, woe betide anyone who attracted his beetle-browed displeasure. Justice is at his irascible best in *Doctor at Sea*, giving arguably his finest performance of the series, mainly because the script gives him so much more to do than in the other entries. He's almost given as much screen time as Bogarde and the film benefits enormously. There's one priceless moment when two crew hands, looking battered and bruised, are brought into his cabin on a charge of fighting and being drunk. At his most benign Justice announces, "First of all, I want to make one thing perfectly clear to you two – you're going to get a completely fair hearing this morning. You're quite at liberty to ask questions of me or any of the other officers and you may call witnesses in your defence. As far as I'm concerned a man's innocent until he's proved guilty. Do you hear that?"

"Yes sir," say the two men.

Justice settles into his chair, still all sweetness and light. "Very well now, tell me your version of the story."

"Well sir," one of the men begins. "It was like this here sir: me and my mate were having a cup of tea..."

Justice bolts to his feet and erupts like a volcano. "You flaming liar, you were rotten drunk – both of you!"

"What, me sir?" the man protests.

"Course you were," continues the tirade. "And don't answer back or I'll kick you round the fo'cstle! Cup of tea indeed. What do you take me for? I was at sea when you were playing marbles in the filth of the gutter with the marks of the cradle hardly off your... You were soused, you miserable scousers. You know what I'd like to do with you? I'd like to clap you in irons in the chain locker on bread and water till we get back to port. I'd like to lash you to the main mast and flog the living hide off you, that's the sort of treatment you scum deserve. You dozy, idle, loafing, illegitimate cutthroats!" Silence falls on the cabin. "Alright," says Justice finally. "Fined five shillings. Good morning." It's a blistering tirade worthy of a De Niro or a Pacino and one of Justices' great screen moments.

Doctor at Sea was chosen as the official British entry at the 1955 Venice Film Festival. The Royal Navy even sent HMS Sheffield to anchor off the Lido to add to Britain's prestige on the night the film was shown. Afterwards cast and crew were invited aboard and royally entertained. But when everybody was leaving, almost as dawn was breaking, nobody could find Richard Gordon anywhere. It was Ralph Thomas who finally uncovered the lost writer, stretched out in a bathtub fast asleep, with his head on a pillow of towels and blissfully unaware that the dripping tap had considerably dampened his dinner jacket. How he got there they never did discover.[11]

It was during the making of another 1955 film, *An Alligator Named Daisy* that actress Diana Dors unearthed yet another one of Justice's (by now) famous hidden talents! Prior to being an actress, Dors had worked for a few years in a typing pool. This came up in conversation during a break in shooting one day when Justice piped up, "I bet I can beat you, I bet I can type faster than you". "Don't be daft James" laughed Dors "I typed for years, professionally". But Justice wasn't impressed and carried on. "Let's put you to the test then, woman. How about a race". That was it, the gauntlet was laid. A date, time and venue were chosen (in a film company production office on the Charing Cross Road) and the two typists duly arrived. With the two adjudicators present they were shown to their desks and, fingers poised, asked to begin. Within two minutes though, Dors had stopped. Not because she had finished the work but because she was actually in a state of shock. Sitting next to her was an eighteen stone Scotsman typing with such speed and ferocity that he resembled an out-of-control bearded express train! Amazed that Justice could even get his fingers on the keys, let alone type, Dors just sat, open-mouthed in a state of both admiration and fear. After another minute or so, Justice stopped. His work was checked and found to be word perfect, not one mistake.

Of course, it's for a string of British pictures, mainly comedies made in the 50s and 60s, that Justice will be forever remembered. However, he was

"Comfy?" JRJ relaxes on Diana Dors during a break in filming 'An Alligator Named Daisy', (1955). This was probably taken before the "typing" incident.

persuaded occasionally to appear in the odd Hollywood production, perhaps most notably *Land of the Pharaohs* (1955), one of the better sand and sandal epics that came conveyor belt style out of tinsel town.

Actually shot on location in Luxor, the Valley of the Kings and Giza, Justice plays enslaved architect Vashtar, who is ordered by a Pharaoh obsessed with life after death to build a magnificent pyramid. Fearing grave robbers, the Pharaoh wants it constructed in such a way that no one can steal the vast treasure that he plans to take with him into the afterlife. Vashtar agrees, on condition that once the structure is built, his people will be set free.

Complications arise when Nellifer, the Pharaoh's wife, played by a young Joan Collins, already in training for her scheming Alexis Carrington role in TV's ultra soap *Dynasty*, assassinates her husband in a bid to gain the Pharaoh's kingdom and all its riches. When the Pharaoh is sealed in his tomb by a fascinating series of sand-operated weights, levers and pulleys, Collins watches in barely controlled glee, oblivious to the Egyptian custom of entombing the Pharaoh's widow alive, along with her husband's body. It's an ironic come-uppance and one of the film's strengths that it ends on such a grim finale.

Extravagantly produced with a large cast and some 10,000 extras, one has to say that of all the male actors, Justice is the most comfortable in the Biblical costume, being, as he was, a fond wearer of the kilt. He also lends the film much needed gravitas and pathos in between scenery chewing appearances by Miss Collins. Jack Hawkins as the Pharaoh looks distinctly uncomfortable and later resented his appearance in the film. The gruff British actor, usually associated with war pictures in which he invariably appeared looking through binoculars on a ship's bridge, had only agreed to appear in this "perfectly ridiculous"[12] film, because he believed that the great American writer, William Faulkner, had penned the screenplay. Unfortunately Faulkner, on being hired for a hefty fee, duly absconded to Paris and his contribution to the script was pared down when other writers were hired for re-writes. Producer/director Howard Hawks later excused the film's somewhat stilted dialogue because, "nobody knew how a Pharaoh talked!"[13] The critics were less than forgiving and gave it the thumbs down, as did audiences, making the film a resounding flop.

Hawks, who had been one of the top directors in the glory days of Hollywood, churning out classic after classic (*Dawn Patrol, Scarface, Bringing up Baby, Sergeant York*) was so distraught by the reaction to *Land of the Pharaohs* that it was another four years before he got behind a camera again, directing the classic John Wayne western *Rio Bravo*.

After their stiff upper lip heroics in *Scott of the Antarctic* Justice and John Mills were reunited in 1955, this time for a bit of classic wartime adventure. *Above us the Waves* charts the true story of the daring attempt to sink the German battleship Tirpitz, anchored in a Norwegian fjord, using midget one-man submarines with explosives strapped to them. The submarines had to travel at least 1,000 miles from base, negotiate a minefield, dodge nets, gun defences and enemy listening posts. Having eluded all these hazards the team placed their charges underneath the ship where they detonated an hour later, doing so much damage that Tirpitz was put out of action for several months. The Tirpitz was subsequently sunk by a bomb especially designed for the job by inventor Sir Barnes Wallis.

Justice has precious little to do in the film as Admiral Ryder, save from give Mills the nod to go ahead and blow up the battleship. But no doubt, the subject matter was close to his heart as several of the crew that took part in the real operation heralded from the RNVR.

Above us the Waves was a real departure for Ralph Thomas, a filmmaker more noteworthy for his frivolous comedies, including, of course, the *Doctor* films,

As General Burroughs in Zoltan Korda's 1955 film, 'Storm Over the Nile'

but he equips himself well here, conveying the claustrophobia of the submarines and the mounting tension leading to the destruction of their intended target. The black and white photography certainly adds to the documentary feel of the whole enterprise. This is one of those refreshing Second World War films where there's no romance bolted on and the Germans actually speak German.

Mills is exceptional as the leader in one of those stiff upper lip roles that would come to be parodied in years to come. And he's ably supported by a band

JRJ introduces his Bonelli's Eagle to a very careful looking Anthony Steel, on the set of 'Storm Over the Nile', 1955

of dependable Brits in the form of Donald Sinden and John Gregson. Look out too for one of Justice's co-stars from *Vice Versa*, Anthony Newley, before he embarked upon his successful singer/songwriting career.

War time heroics from a different age next for Justice when he appeared in *Storm over the Nile*, which was not so much a remake of Zoltan Korda's classic *The Four Feathers*, but something of a pillage, as most of its grand-scale battle scenes was merely footage lifted from the 1939 film. Obviously this was done for budgetary reasons, a shame really since the director was Terence Young, a man more than capable of creating great action on screen, as would be seen later in his career when he was asked to direct three out of the four early *James Bond* movies.

A.E.W. Mason's novel is arguably the epitome of the Boy's Own adventure. It tells the story of British officer Harry Faversham, who resigns his commission from his regiment just prior to them heading out to fight in the Sudanese campaign of the late 1890s. He does this for his own personal reasons, rather than cowardice. However, he is faced with censure from three of his comrades for cowardice (signified by the delivery of three white feathers to him) and the loss of the support of his fiancée, who presents him with the fourth feather. He questions his own true motives, and resolves to redeem himself in combat, travelling on his own to the Sudan.

Justice receives third billing to the two leading men, Anthony Steel and Laurence Harvey, playing a snuff-taking old general. Besides a rather bad dye job to grey his hair and beard, Justice is a good replacement for C. Aubrey Smith, who played the same character in the earlier version. He was only in his late forties by this time, but still manages to convince as a much older man, instilling Churchillian gruffness into his voice, as he bores anyone within listening range about his exploits as a soldier during the Crimean war. He recalls how one fellow, "lost his arm – ruined his cricket" and re-enacts the famous battle of Balaclava at the dining table with himself represented by a pineapple! It's a great comic moment.

Another picture from what was possibly Justice's most hectic filmmaking period was *Out of the Clouds* (1955), another Ealing production. The studio had become the most respected and successful in the post-war era, but their dramatic efforts had always tended to pale by comparison with their more famous comedies and *Out of the Clouds* is no exception, despite the presence of several regular players, including Justice. This is a rather dull compendium of personal stories set against the backdrop of a fogbound London Airport, when mass tourism had yet to hit the skies. Justice plays Captain Dougie Brent, a veteran pilot, whose doubts about a new aircraft prove to be well-founded. Other one-dimensional characters popping up are Anthony Steel's pilot with a chronic gambling weakness, Canadian ex-pat Robert Beatty, grounded through ill health, desperate to take to the skies again, and the obligatory airline hostess love interest. Watch out, in minor roles, for the likes of Bernard Lee (not yet M in the *James Bond* films) as a custom's officer and Sid James as an American gambler.

Maybe in 1955 all this seemed quite original, but after Arthur Hailey's treatment of the same formula in the 1960's with his novel *Airport*, and the subsequent disaster movie series and their later parodies, *Out of the Clouds* looks remarkably tame, almost a museum piece; it's main point of interest today, thanks to Paul Beeson's Eastman Colour photography, is as a fascinating record of how Heathrow looked in its early days.

Despite only receiving fifth billing, as well as struggling with a fairly pale script, Justice manages to grab all the scenes he is in; even managing to call his aeroplane a 'cow' – rather risqué for the time. *Out of the Clouds* was directed by Basil Dearden who would go on to bigger and better things with the classic

British caper movie *The League of Gentleman*, the Dirk Bogarde drama *Victim* and the epic *Khartoum*. Sadly the same couldn't be said for Ealing. Within a few years the studios would be no more and consigned to film history, although its finer works still remain cherished by many as the true classics they are.

[1]   Box, Betty E. *'Lifting The Lid'* – The Book Guild (2000)

[2]   Interview with Ralph Thomas, Classic Images, March 1996

[3]   Author interview with Betty Box at Pinewood Studios – 1994

[4]   Box, Betty E. *'Lifting The Lid'* – The Book Guild (2000) p113

[5]   Ibid, p114

[6]   Author interview with Betty Box at Pinewood Studios – 1994

[7]   Box, Betty E. *'Lifting The Lid'* – The Book Guild (2000) – p108

[8]   Ibid

[9]   Ibid, p111

[10] Ibid, p112

[11] Ibid, p116

[12] McCarthy, Todd *'Howard Hawks: The Grey Fox of Hollywood'* (Grove – 2000) p 530

[13] Ibid, p520

Footnote:

On 17th October 1955 Justice was Roy Plomley's guest on *Desert Island Discs*. We understand that the programme itself no longer exists. However, we did manage to find out which pieces of music Justice chose for the show and have listed them below.

1 Monteverdi's 'Vespro della Beata Vergine', sung by Swabian Choral Singers/Stuttgart Bach

2 Bach's Unaccompanied Partita No 2 in D minor, played by Yehudi Menuhin, *violin*

3 Beethoven's Quartet in A minor (opus 132, beginning of 2nd movement), played by Busch Quartet

4 Beethoven's Quartet in A minor (opus 132, beginning of 3rd movement, played by Busch Quartet

5 Beethoven's Quartet in A minor (opus 132, another part of 3rd movement, played by Busch Quartet

6 Bartók, Piano Concerto No 2 (Edith Farnadi/Vienna State Orchestra/Scherchen)

7 Recording of the call of a flock of pink-footed geese

8 'The Flowers of the Forest' (lament) (John Burgess/*Scottish Highland Bagpipes*)

Luxury object: A packet of mixed seeds of the flowers one grows at home.

CHAPTER 16:
HELLO MOLLY

During this run of film success, Justice and Dilys remained married. They had supported each other through the tragedy of the drowning of their son, but clearly the incident had an impact on their relationship and although the subject of divorce never arose, Justice began several affairs and saw other women.

One romantic tryst was with Molly Parkin, who would become an iconic fashion journalist of the 'Swinging Sixties'. It brought this young woman the admiration of her parents and the prospect of marriage. Apparently, Justice was keen to start another family but Parkin was happy in her single life and turned down his proposal. Still, she later remembered Justice in her autobiography as the, "most formative influence in my life."[1]

Their first introduction was by telephone when Justice rang to invite her flatmate out for dinner. She wasn't there, so Justice took Molly out instead and the whirlwind romance began. Molly knew Justice was married and loved his wife dearly but, almost immediately, he wanted to set up home with her in London, to buy her a house and start a family together, so that she could give him another son. Instead of feeling overjoyed by Justice's proposal, the secrecy of their affair triggered off an unsettling anxiety within her and a heavy dose of guilt.[2]

Justice was then almost fifty, "but at his peak," Molly wrote. "In his prime. I thrilled to the potent male power of him." However she was less than enthralled at the prospect of Justice driving her to the secondary school where she taught art. The very first time he did, dropping her off on his way to Pinewood Studios, where he was filming, Molly pleaded with him to park around the corner. She didn't want anyone to see her with a man at that time of the morning, let alone with the famous James Robertson Justice. "They might jump to all sorts of conclusions and think there was something going on!" which indeed there was! "He ignored the pleas, throwing his large head back and guffawing at my obvious discomfort. But let's face it, the sheer gut-churning glamour of sitting in a sports car with a film star. Fuck what people would say!"[3]

Far from being inconspicuous Justice screeched to a halt, halfway up the kerb at the very edge of the school playground attracting, not surprisingly, a horde of gaping girls who flung themselves all over the bonnet. To get rid of them Justice gave one blast of his horn, but this only succeeded in attracting more, which actually delighted him. To escape further embarrassment Molly jumped out of the car, dreading the farewell embrace she knew he was planning for the benefit of the over-excited audience, she instead gave a hasty wave from the school gates as he swung the car around and zoomed off. Not surprisingly Molly's pupils gave her hell all day.[4]

Justice was shooting *Doctor at Sea* at the time and confessed to Molly that every week he was reminded of her body while working, and one day was so overcome that he almost forgot his lines. "There's this French girl on the set who has breasts just like yours," he told her. Year's later Molly saw the film and recognised the French girl as Brigitte Bardot.[5]

Ironically, Molly's father was a regular filmgoer and James Robertson Justice was one of his faves. "I longed to tell him that his idol was screwing his daughter until the cows came home," Molly later wrote. "That on our very first date we dined at the Ivy, with stars of stage, screen and radio at every table. And there, within inches of everyone, James had his fingers in my Marks & Spencer knickers under the table, almost all through the meal."[6]

That very night they made love for the first time in a suite in the Cadogan Hotel. No sooner had the couple entered the lift than Justice started kissing her and amorously tore off her knickers in the corridor and tossed them in the fire bucket. Hours later, when Molly sneaked out to retrieve them she was dismayed to discover someone had stolen them. "I was surprised. You'd expect better than a bunch of thieving perverts in the middle of Belgravia."[7]

Justice would become much more than a sexual partner, but a mentor of sorts, teaching Molly how to think for herself, encouraging her to read more widely, giving her, for example, Dylan Thomas's *Under Milkwood*, for her journey to work. He said that poetic prose and pornography were the perfect travelling companions, in life as on a journey.

Soon the novelty of her affair grew stale. Molly's friends were marrying men of their own age group, while she was stuck, hanging about when Justice was off on location, filming. "Like any girl in an affair with a married man, I had to sit tight and keep mum, taking what I could get." Molly was to learn the hard way that it was a mug's game; too painful a lesson on which to waste her youth. But she was unable to break away.[8]

When Molly's parents visited her in London, to see for themselves how their daughter was getting on, they were having a cup of tea in her flat before going out, when the telephone rang. Molly was dreading it would be Justice, checking she was at home on Saturday night and not out night clubbing. Molly's father answered, putting on a mock posh voice. "This is the London residence of Molly Thomas. The butler speaking. Who shall I say is calling?"

Justice was not happy to hear a male voice and exploded: "Who the fuck's this? Tell the tart that it's James and to get her bloody arse over to this telephone!"

Molly's father baulked at such language, particularly as it was directed at his own daughter: "James who exactly?"

The answer thundered back. "James Robertson Justice, of course, you bloody ignorant little swine! What other James would it be for Christ's sake?"

"*The* James Robertson Justice?" Molly sensed her father was about to enter embarrassment overload and saw her mother swinging her arms about in excitement, too. "Allow me this opportunity, as Molly's father, sir, of saying what an enormous pleasure your performances have afforded me in the past. I know my good lady wife wishes to join me in my sentiments. Here she is, sir, to have a bit of a word herself. I'm putting her on…." Molly could take it no longer and left the room.[9]

Molly admits that she wasn't entirely faithful to Justice; she had been seeing other men, also many years her senior. Curiously when her father died, in his mid-fifties, her taste for older men withered and died and she finished with every single one of them, including Justice. Molly never saw him again.[10]

[1-10] Parkin, Molly '*Moll: Making of Molly Parkin*' (Gollancz – 1994)

JRJ with Belinda Lee and June Thorburn at Hamburg Airport. Two extremely talented actresses who both died tragically young. 1956. (University of Hamburg/Conti Press)

CHAPTER 17:
EDUCATING McJUSTICE

Whilst enjoying considerable success as a film personality, Justice's public profile was heightened further with guest appearances on popular BBC radio shows of the period. His first major role was as Archie Andrews' new tutor, in the extremely popular *Educating Archie*.

Educating Archie was one of the more significant radio programmes of its era, turning gifted, but relatively unknown beginners into stars. Initially given only a twelve-week run in 1950, *Educating Archie* ran for ten years and had regular audiences of over twelve million listeners. Robert Moreton played Archie's first tutor, and was followed by such luminaries as Tony Hancock, Gilbert Harding, Bruce Forsyth, Sid James and then Justice himself in 1955. Other regular cast members included Max Bygraves as the odd-job man and Hattie Jacques as Agatha Dinglebody. A young girl soprano, only thirteen, was the resident singer. Her name was Julie Andrews.

A BBC Audience Research Report dated 30th September 1955 and conducted after the transmission of Justice's first appearance on the show reported that the actor had amassed much favourable comment. "Some, however, were obviously not too happy about the choice of James Robertson Justice,"[1] stated the report. They said that he seemed out of his element, and not comfortable in his role. They regarded him as a straight actor, and found it strange to hear him in a variety show of this kind. This is really hardly the métier

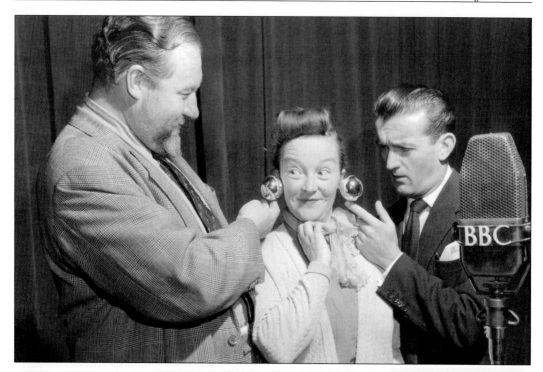

Top: JRJ and Graham Stark admire Beryl Reid's earrings, prior to a recording of Educating Archie – September 1955. Bottom: JRJ and Peter Scott discuss the programme at the International Nature and Wildlife Film Festival in 1955 at which they were both invited to speak. (The Scotsman)

Left: JRJ and June Thorburn arrive in Hamburg for the opening of The Streit Cinema, owned by The Rank Organisation. The Streit was Rank's first cinema in Germany and to celebrate they flew out some of their biggest stars, including Donald Sinden, Peter Finch, Belinda Lee and Muriel Pavlow. December 1956. Right: JRJ goes through Belinda Lee's luggage at Hamburg Airport, December 1956 (University of Hamburg).

for such a fine actor. The majority, however, were definitely in favour of this new appointment: "Here at last is somebody to keep the irascible Archie in order."[2] Listeners generally admired the way he entered into the spirit of the programme. His rich voice and clear diction were a delight, and although a few accused him of trying to copy Gilbert Harding, others said they found his irascibility most enjoyable to listen to. Said another housewife – "I think he is a splendid addition to the team. One can't help wondering though, if he really acts, or is just being himself? Either way, the result is perfect!"[3]

Another highlight of Justice's radio career was a guest spot in *Hancock's Half Hour*. In the episode 'The Last of the McHancocks,' broadcast in February 1957, he played the wonderfully named McNasty of McNasty. But Justice's all too brief career in radio soon ended, barely two years after it had begun, by which time he was making more than enough money in films.

One such picture saw him re-united once again with Gregory Peck. Having ridden tempestuous waters already with the Hollywood star in the role of a famous sea captain, Justice happily signed on as crewmember once again, but this time with a big difference. Peck had been asked to play the vengeful Captain Ahab in John Huston's version of Herman Melville's classic novel about the white whale, *Moby Dick*. Conceived wisdom is that Peck is woefully miscast in the role (he probably is and said himself that Huston should have played it)[4], but there's no question that Huston's darkly brooding film is the best, if perhaps slightly flawed, version of this oft told tale.

Justice's performance is little more than a cameo, as Captain Boomer, a rival whaler with a vicious hook on the end of one arm – "Better than flesh and blood," he roars merrily. Justice's appearance is not the only cameo as actor-director Orson Welles also turns up. Welles puts on a magnificent show as Father Mapple, climbing into his pulpit, via rigging not steps, that is shaped like the prow of a sailing vessel. Heavily made up, he cuts a striking figure, even before he speaks.

While some location work was carried out in the Canary Islands and around the coast of Ireland, most of the film was shot at Shepperton and Elstree Studios in 1956. The biggest headache facing Huston was the whale itself. A giant 60 foot model was built and filmed on the open sea, but it kept sinking and breaking up and had to be continuously rebuilt, leading to budget overruns and schedule delays. Most of the whales appearing in the finished film are various sized miniatures and are still eerily effective today.

From high adventure to comedy next with *The Iron Petticoat* (1956), yet another Betty Box/Ralph Thomas production. Justice, who seemed to be their one-man rep company, was asked to participate, though he probably wished he could have given this one a miss.

The signs looked good: two BIG imported American stars for once in the shape of Bob Hope and Katherine Hepburn. So many British films of this period brought over B movie American leads to feebly make their films attractive to the US market. Box and Thomas had also shrewdly hired the great Hollywood screenwriter Ben Hecht, who had hoped to engage Cary Grant for the male lead. When Grant turned the role down and Hope was assigned as Hepburn's comic foil, Hecht was far from happy. He was even more pissed off when Hope brought over his own gang of writers to punch up the screenplay and tailor it to his own style, in the process cutting out several of his co-star's best scenes, and turning the whole thing into just another comedy vehicle for Bob Hope. Far from being the star, Hepburn, one of Hollywood's greatest actresses, was sidelined as little more than Hope's straight man, or feed. William K. Zinzeer, of the *New York Herald-Tribune*, complained that, "When Miss Hepburn... turns to Hope and says, 'I vas vorried,' she had good reason."[5] Eventually Hecht insisted that his name be removed from the credits, and printed an open letter in the film trade journals disclaiming the picture and offering Hepburn and her fans an apology.

The Iron Petticoat owes much of its inspiration to that great Greta Garbo comedy *Ninotchka*, but it's not in the same league – nay the same universe.

Aus Anlaß

der Eröffnung des

Filmtheaters in Streit's Haus

gibt sich

Mr. John Davis,

Generaldirektor der Rank Organisation,

die Ehre,

Sie zu einem Empfang

im Anschluß an die

Eröffnungs-Vorstellung

um 24 Uhr im Alsterpavillon

einzuladen

An advert from the German newspaper Hamburger Abendblatt publicising the opening of The Streit Cinema in Hamburg, which opened with 'Doctor at Sea' in December 1956. (University of Hamburg)

Hepburn plays Captain Vinka Kovelenko, a Russian pilot who lands in West Germany. After defecting she is quickly converted to capitalism after sampling life in the West in the company of Major Chuck Lockwood (Hope). Justice turns up periodically (thank God, too) as the barking, grumpy Russian bigwig who desperately tries to reclaim Hepburn from the clutches of imperialist decadence. To this end he employs Hepburn's timid ex-boyfriend, played by renowned ballet dancer Robert Helpmann – cue lots of in-jokes about his inability to dance. Helpmann, of course, would go on to appear with Justice as the creepy Child Catcher in *Chitty Chitty Bang Bang*. When Helpmann fails, Justice deploys a collection of dedicated Communist misfits, chief among their number a certain Sid James, wearing a very odd semi-Mohican hairpiece.

The Iron Petticoat opened at the Berlin Film Festival before swiftly disappearing from the public's attention. Justice was soon back on familiar comedy ground in *Doctor at Large*, the third entry in Betty Box/Ralph Thomas' now hugely successful *Doctor* series. Light-hearted throughout, it's an agreeably undemanding comedy designed to appeal right across the board, dealing with

As Colonel Sklarnoff in the poorly received Hope/Hepburn comedy, 'The Iron Petticoat', 1956

the further madcap exploits of Dr Simon Sparrow (Dirk Bogarde); in particular his attempts at general practice.

The cast of British dependables is very good and the film immeasurably benefits from the presence once more of Justice as the overbearing Sir Lancelot Spratt, who by this stage had turned the character into one of the most memorable in British comedy history, "James made Sir Lancelot so real because he fitted the part," says Richard Gordon. "And the part fitted him. James knew his job and how to do it, like any good surgeon. He was large, snuff sniffing, impressive and assertive, though a film's unit, unlike Sir Lancelot's students, could answer him back. His one professional failing was an inability to remember his lines. Before auto-cues, this required writing them in capitals across a long white banner, hoisted on sticks over the camera crew."[6]

Leslie Phillips also recalls Justice's anathema towards learning his lines. "He always hated learning lines but made no excuses. He simply pasted chunks of script wherever he could read them – on his arm or, in one case, the underside of the bunk he was lying beneath – in fact, anywhere convenient. Ralph Thomas handled him beautifully. If James didn't feel like doing what he'd been asked, he would roar, "Bloody hell, man! I'm not doing that!' But somehow Ralph always quietly got what he wanted."[7]

Missing from *Doctor at Sea*, Bogarde's beau from the first film, Muriel Pavlow, returned for *Large*, happy to do so, but at the same time feeling that this third instalment didn't quite have the same magic. "I remember Dirk saying to me that we would have to work a bit harder on this one as we wouldn't have Kenny More's wonderful spirit. He was right. I wouldn't say the later films didn't work, because they did, but there was a certain something that the first one had that wasn't in the others. The ingredients and casting in *Doctor in the House* were sheer perfection and, like a good soufflé, it rose beautifully. That was certainly the benchmark film."[8]

Harbouring similar thoughts Bogarde was keen to move away from his Simon Sparrow character and pursue more challenging roles. A replacement would have to be found for the next film.

[1] BBC Audience Research Report, Educating Archie, Friday 30th September 1955

[2] Ibid

[3] Ibid

[4] Source unknown

[5] *New York Herald-Tribune* – 4th January 1957

[6] Letters to author from Richard Gordon – 2005

[7] Phillips, Leslie 'Hello' (Orion – 2006), p221-222

[8] Cinema Retro Magazine (2007)

A signed photo given to his nephew, Jamie in the late 1950's. It must have had some effect as Jamie has since gone on to become an accomplished piper himself.

CHAPTER 18:
RECTOR IN THE HOUSE

In November 1957, Justice was elected Rector of Edinburgh University – an achievement that provided him with enormous pride. When he delivered his rectorial address at his installation in the McEwan Hall on Thursday, 20th February 1958 with the chancellor of the university, Prince Philip present, he extolled the virtues of education, believing that teachers were undervalued in society and that they should have more respect.[1]

On the same day, *The Student*, Edinburgh University's student magazine published a 'Special Installation Issue', with a kilted Justice on the front cover, as he stood proudly outside his Scottish home.

Patrick Hamilton, as President of the Student Union, was responsible for the installation of Justice as Rector, and appointed Martin Leslie to be in charge of the security for the event. Justice was staying with Compton MacKenzie during his Edinburgh trip and after a preliminary meeting which finished at 9.30pm one night, asked the two lads if they had ever met the famous writer. "No" was the reply. "And to our astonishment and concern," says Leslie, "James invited us to come and meet him – we reckoned it was far too late! We went in some trepidation but were welcomed into a small study where there was a nice fire and only two arm chairs – one occupied by Compton MacKenzie, the other soon occupied by James! Patrick and I were given large glasses of whisky and invited to sit on the floor. We sat in rapt silence while the two men knocked sparks off each other as they reminisced and discussed all manner of subjects. Our attempts to get up and leave resulted in more whisky and being told to sit down! We got away at about midnight and had some trouble finding something to eat as we walked home – neither of us had had anything to eat since lunch!"[2]

After the successful installation, Justice organised a lunch for all those involved with running the Rectorial on the following Saturday. Leslie said he could not attend as he was playing rugby for his College on one of the back pitches at Murrayfield with a 2.30pm kick off and so would never get there in time – the lunch was held in the Surgeon's Hall on the other side of Edinburgh! "James considered this to be a weak excuse and ordered me, in his capacity as Rector, to attend his lunch! He would pay for a taxi to stand by and get me to the match on time! It was an amazing lunch, with wonderful wine, and I was then put in the taxi with my rugby kit, a half smoked cigar and yet another glass of brandy! Arriving at Murrayfield, I somehow got changed and out onto the pitch 10 minutes after the match had started! My team-mates were not impressed when, having reported to the referee, I took my place on the wing still smoking the cigar! I remember little of the match, was told I had never played better, and was never so stiff and sore for days afterwards! Patrick reported his friend's state of health to James with considerable glee! When I saw James later in the summer he had a good chuckle remarking that he was surprised that I survived the match to its end as he had been determined that his hospitality should have a 'beneficial' effect and has asked Patrick to see to it"[3]

Justice took his position as Rector extremely seriously. Really it was up to the individual concerned what sort of responsibilities went with the position. The official duties were minimal. "The amount you put into it is an arrangement you make with yourself,"[4] he said. Justice knew that in the past a great number of rectors, distinguished Prime Ministers and so on had merely turned up, delivered an inaugural and always political speech and then weren't seen again until they turned up to collect an honorary degree at the end of their term.

So what contribution did Justice wish to bring to Edinburgh University? "By taking a considerable interest in the welfare of the undergraduate body,[5] he said. "The Rector is second only to the Chancellor, who is the senior figure of the University. The rector is in fact the representative of the student body. The rector in all continental Universities has the most enchanting title because he's always addressed as Your Magnificence. Unfortunately we haven't got this in Scotland which is a shame because I rather like the idea of being addressed as Your Magnificence!"[6]

Such was Justice's pride in his new position that he wrote to Dilys' sister and her husband, Olwyn and James Thomson, in Canada, from where he had only just

Top: With Steve Forrest and Liliane Montevecchi in 'The Living Idol', 1957. Bottom: Michael Medwin tries (and fails) to talk his way out of trouble in 'Doctor at Large', 1957

Top: With (left to right) Richard Gordon (author of the Doctor books), Terence Longden and Dirk Bogarde in 'Doctor at Large', 1957 . Bottom: JRJ with Paul Massie in the 1958 Anthony Asquith film, 'Orders to Kill'

Top Left: As James MacDonald in 'Campbell's Kingdom', 1957. Centre Left: Phillip Glasier, Gavin Maxwell and The Duke of Edinburgh, on the moors near Spinningdale in the late 1950's. (Martin Leslie). Bottom Left: "Oh lucky Jim!" JRJ enjoys a role in the hay with the beautiful François Arnoul in the French film, 'Thérèse Étienne', 1958

Top Right: A publicity shot for the Box/Thomas film, 'Campbell's Kingdom', 1957. Bottom Right: Relaxing at Spinningdale, 1958 (Stephen Frank)

Top: JRJ with Paul Massie in 'Orders to Kill'. Bottom: JRJ with Dilys' sister, Olwyn and her family at Vancouver Airport in 1958. One of the books' major contributors, JRJ's nephew Jamie, is on the far left. (Jamie Thomson)

returned after film promotion duties, offering his insights into the inauguration ceremony: "I got back to Edinburgh on the Sunday feeling more dead than alive, and had to sit down to write seven and a half thousand words of reasonably intelligent material to deliver on the Thursday, but all things considered it went very well, and I managed to keep the audience more or less under control."[7]

Justice then revealed that his friend, Prince Philip, whom he refers to in the letter as 'Young Master' was also in attendance, presiding over the ceremony, acting in his capacity as the University's Chancellor. "I may say that the Young Master did me jolly proud, for at the university dinner afterwards, when I was so tired I didn't really know what I was doing, he proposed a toast to the Rector, roughly speaking as follows: 'You may realise that I have to perform this sort of job quite frequently. It is always a pleasure to propose the health of distinguished and eminent persons, but more especially is it a pleasure on this occasion, when the person whose health I propose happens also to be my old and valued friend.' Well you can't say fairer than that."[8]

Once the formalities were completed, Prince Philip, Justice and Compton Mackenzie retired to Mackenzie's home nearby for some welcome refreshment. "It was imperative to conceal the Duke's visit from reporters and cameramen for his own relaxation," Mackenzie recalled. "We were successful in keeping the secret and while (they) were chasing one clue after another all over Edinburgh, the Duke and the new Rector of the University was enjoying an old malt whisky...uncorked for the occasion."[9]

At the time Prince Charles attended a boys' prep school in London, where he was treated like any other pupil of his age. Now, though, at the age of 12, he'd reached a stage when the vacation-time company of his 10-year old sister Anne was clearly not enough for him. His father understandably spent a great deal of time away from home so, on the few occasions when James wasn't filming, he'd allow his son a short stay at Spinningdale.[10]

Justice seemed such an unlikely companion for a royal Prince but Charles thought a lot of him. With Justice having lost his own son in a tragic accident, this may in part explain the strong bond that formed so naturally between them. Betty Box saw it clearly: "James was one of the most diversely knowledgeable of men. His skill with falcons is widely known, but I don't think many people realise that when in Scotland he spent some of his time passing on to young Prince Charles his knowledge and love of wildlife. James would have made a wonderful teacher, and it saddened me to think of the tragedy which lost him his only child. But when I watched James with the young Charles, I knew how he must have grieved at his loss. He treated the Prince like an adult and they appeared to understand each other well."[11]

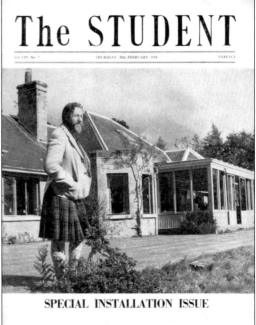

Top: Students of Edinburgh University carry a triumphant JRJ to McEwan Hall, where he was officially installed as Rector on 20th February 1958 (The Scotsman). Centre Left: The Duke of Edinburgh (Chancellor of Edinburgh University) congratulates JRJ after his installation. (The Scotsman). Bottom Left: JRJ gives his Rectorial address in the McEwan Hall at Edinburgh University (The Scotsman). Above: A Special Installation Issue of Edinburgh University's student publication, The Student, was produced to celebrate JRJ's first term as Rector (Mike Farmer)

Top: JRJ attends his installation dinner as Rector of Edinburgh University in February 1958. Second left is Jo Grimond, the then leader of the Liberal Party who was preceded and succeeded by Justice as Rector. (The Scotsman) Bottom: JRJ in a horse drawn carriage taking part in the Edinburgh University charities week procession – April 1959. (The Scotsman)

On his visits to Spinningdale Martin Leslie often saw the Duke and went hawking with him and Justice. "We were hawking up there one day and it was absolutely roasting hot and, quite suddenly, Prince Philip said, 'Right, come-on, we're all going for a swim in the loch.' You haven't seen people disappear so fast. The entire company, of which there were four or five, disappeared. And his beady eye fixed upon me. 'You're not lily-livered like those others, I can tell. Come-on, we'll go in together.' Everybody else in the party had bolted save for Justice, and he was adamant he wasn't going in and instead pointed at me. 'HE'LL go in!' I had no choice. I stripped-off, it was like liquid ice and I could see Prince Philip saying, 'Good lord, if it's that cold I don't think I'll go in either!' I thought James was going to have a seizure, he laughed so hard. We had a lot of happy times."[12]

Leslie had also been there when the young Prince and sometimes Princess Anne visited, this at the time when Anne was six, and the young Prince Charles eight. "It was lovely to see the way Prince Philip treated his children in the same way that any father treats their children. He made them help Cathy clear the table of plates and then to go and do the washing-up. And when bedtime came in the evening he was the chap who oversaw their bath routine and read to them and tucked them down before they went to sleep."[13]

[1] Taken from The Rectorial Address of Dr James Robertson Justice – delivered in the McEwan Hall at Edinburgh University, 20th February 1958

[2] Author interview with Martin Leslie – Isle of Skye – 2007

[3] Ibid

[4] Interview with Joan Bakewell – BBC Television – 1966 – last shown in 2004 as part of BBC4's 1960's season.

[5] Ibid

[6] Ibid

[7] Letter written 14th February 1958. Courtesy of Jamie Thomson.

[8] Ibid

[9] Carol, David 'Edinburgh: Literary Lives & Landscapes' (Sutton Publishing – 2004, p124

[10] Hotchkiss, Christine – Vancouver Sun – Date unknown

[11] Box, Betty E. 'Lifting The Lid' – The Book Guild (2000) – p 113

[12] Author interview with Martin Leslie – Isle of Skye – 2007

[13] Ibid

CHAPTER 19:
THE GREAT IRINA

In 1960, during the filming of an otherwise totally forgettable film about Clare Booth Luce, the American author and US diplomat, Justice met and fell in love with the woman who would change his life completely – the German film star Irina von Meyendorff. Justice insisted that he had wooed his future wife, "in an eloquent but antiquated German learnt from an elderly Prussian Princess."[1] Balderdash of course, no doubt he'd picked up his lovemaking German while a student at Bonn. "He did of course spend a considerable amount of time in Germany and spoke absolute fluent German," says Keith Shackleton. "In fact, during a stay down at Slimbridge in 1946, I remember us all seeing a party of German POWs who were working on the nature reserve. James went over to talk to them and I remember that he was with them quite a while. Afterwards, the German officer in charge of the party said that he couldn't understand how James had been able to remain persona-grata with the British. They *genuinely* thought he was a German spy."[2]

The couple's whirlwind romance was such that Irina abandoned her third husband, family and career, in order to live with Justice in Britain. "James gave me something that no German husband ever could," she once explained, "absolute freedom. I never have to hide from him anything that I thought or I did – how could I not love him?"[3]

Justice was still legally bound to Dilys, though they had separated in 1958, and he had sought solace with other women, even being cited in a divorce suit. In October 1961, Justice was ordered to pay the costs of a divorce action in which he was cited as co-respondent by Viscount Lord Savernake (Michael Sydney Cedric Brudenell-Bruce). The Marquess of Aylesbury's son and heir was granted a decree nisi because of the adultery of his wife, 28, with Justice. The petition was not defended. In other words, Justice put his hand up. The adultery was committed at Spinningdale in 1958. Lord Savernake re-married in 1963, and later became the 8th Marquess of Aylesbury.[4]

It would be another eight years after meeting Irina before Justice and Dilys formally divorced in November 1968. The decree was granted to Dilys, then living in Dover, Kent on the grounds of her husband's adultery with Baroness Irina Von Meyerndorff. She was eventually granted a periodical allowance of £50 a week.

By then Justice and Irina were a firm fixture. Just the previous year, in 1967, Irina gained British citizenship and changed her first name from Irene to Irina. But for many of the people who knew her when she lived with Justice, she was always the Baroness.

Even before she met and fell in love with James Robertson Justice, the life of Irina von Meyendorff had already been an extraordinary adventure. She was born Baroness Irene Isabella Margarete Paulina Caecilia von Meyendorff ex den hause Uxkull on 6th June 1916 at Reval (present day Tallinn), the eldest child of Fyodor, her deeply conservative father, and Elisabeth, her passionately liberal mother. This was still Tsarist Russia, and Irina was heiress to vast estates in Estonia conferred on her forebears by Catherine the Great, and apparently destined for a life of aristocratic privilege; but history and fate soon intervened.

While she was still a baby, the Bolshevik revolution of 1917 drove the family into exile. What little wealth they had left – jewellery – was smuggled out in the infant Irene's cot. Next stop, Berlin. Stoically Fyodor found work in the city as a vending-machine attendant and rapidly made a fortune, but by 1924 his wife Elisabeth had run off with a young poet. Irene went with them, to become immersed in the bohemian culture of Weimar Germany. It bred in her a belief in artistic freedom which melded seamlessly with the aristocratic self-confidence of her background. It never truly left her. When she died in 2001, at the age of eighty-five, she'd been married five times.

By the time she met Justice, Irina had been an actress for nearly twenty-five years. As an eighteen-year-old student, with ambitions of becoming a wildlife photographer, she went to train instead at Universum-Film Aktiengesellschaft (UFA), the largest film studio in Germany. Unaware of her own mesmerising beauty – and her good fortune – she was outraged when a sharp-eyed casting

Top: The Prince of Wales (fourth from right) and The Duke of Edinburgh join JRJ for an afternoon's grouse hunting on Birichen Moor in the late 1950's. (Jamie Thomson) Bottom: 'Hunting with Peregrines'
Left to right – Phillip Glasier (swinging a lune to get his Falcon back), June Woodford, The Duke of Edinburgh, JRJ, Stephen Frank and Frederick (The Duke of Edinburgh's Private Protection Officer) holding JRJ's Pointer, Robina on the moors close to Spinningdale in the late 1950's. (Martin Leslie)

Top Left : Out on the moors with his favourite pointer, Robina in the early 1960's. (Martin Leslie) Top Right: JRJ in 1960, sporting his 'British Racing Drivers Club' badge. As far as we know, JRJ is the only actor ever to have gained membership. Bottom: JRJ, thoroughly enjoying himself (as you would!) at an anti-smoking meeting at Central Hall in Tollcross – October 1959 (The Scotsman)

"Happy the Man" – Holding a Peregrine Falcon in the late 1950's.

director spotted her and offered her the lead in the film adaptation of a current best-seller. "What a dreadful suggestion," she exclaimed. "That's the sort of book our servants read."[5]

But UFA persisted, offering her other parts, and in 1935 persuaded her to take the lead in a film called *The Four from Santa Cruz*. Her appeal was immediate, and subsequent roles confirmed her as such a star that she became known simply as Die Meyendorff. Her popularity was due partly to her blonde hair, blue eyes and classic good looks. "I was considered the image of the ideal German woman," she would say dismissively, "pretty, kind, stupid and faithful."[6]

Her rise to stardom coincided with the Nazi's rise to power in the 1930s, a regime not averse to using the cinema for propaganda purposes. Everything in her family background and her bohemian upbringing was hostile to Nazi ideology. The Uxkull family to which she belonged was related to the von Stauffenbergs, and closely involved in the famous plot to assassinate Hitler, and many of her friends were Jewish artists. She had no compunction in rebuffing the advances of Dr Goebbels, who as head of propaganda and ultimately of UFA, was accustomed to having his pick of the studio's actresses. "You would degrade me," Irene said freezingly, "and you would degrade yourself.[7]

"Unfortunately," a dejected Goebbels wrote in his diary, "Fraulein von Meyendorff seems rather cold."[8]

More problematically, her first husband, Heinz Zahler, by whom she had a son, Andreas, born in 1940, and who sadly later committed suicide, was part of a right-wing circle plotting to replace Hitler with a military government. An eminent doctor, Zahler specialised in mood-altering drugs; he himself was a cocaine addict. In 1941 Goering, who needed drugs to suppress his own codeine addiction, appointed him his personal physician. "Now you must kill him," Irene insisted. "You could poison him, and no one would suspect."[9] But soon afterwards, police arrested Zahler for possessing cocaine. Alarmed that he might break down when deprived of the drug, Irene went to Goering and persuaded him to overrule the police and order Zahler's release.

Although she was more popular with the German soldiers than any other actress, Irene's family background and aversion to Nazi ideology led to her being offered fewer roles and when Germany lost the war, she was penniless and in self-imposed exile in Bavaria. With her first marriage on the rocks, she had to begin again. Her second marriage was to film producer, Joachim Matthes, and they made several films together, such as *Gift im Zoo* (1952), but that relationship soon foundered. Her third husband, Pitt Severin, was a Hamburg journalist, but she turned her back on that marriage and celebrity when she embraced her new life with the burly Justice. Effectively she curtailed her acting

Top Left: Scottish artist, Emilio Coia showing off his drawing of JRJ in 1960 (The Scotsman) Top Right: On Birichin Moor in the early 1960's. (Jamie Thomson) Bottom: JRJ, in the garden at Spinningdale in 1958. (Jamie Tompson)

IRENE VON MEYENDORFF

Above Left: JRJ with Irina (then Irene) and Nadja Tiller (centre), in the 1960 German film, 'Die Botschafterin'.
Soon after filming, Irina left her third husband to be with James.

Above Right: An signed publicity photo of Irina from the early 1930's.

Left: One of JRJ's many forays into advertising. This time representing Frigidaire refrigerators in the June 1960 issue of Ideal Home Magazine.

career, although she did appear in the odd film. She was Countess Stockau in Terence Young's epic, *Mayerling* (1968), when Justice played the role of Edward, Prince of Wales.

Besides a home in England, Justice and Irina spent a great deal of time at Spinningdale, creating their very own Camelot where they flew falcons and entertained a variety of friends and, in some cases, almost complete strangers. Guests included renowned falconers, naturalists, students and writers, even foreign royalty, including the then ruler of Abu Dhabi, Sheikh Shakhbut Bin-

Sultan Al Nahyan. Everybody was made welcome to enjoy the moors and grouse in equal measure. All were encouraged to experiment with exotic raptors, such as shahins, lanners and sakers – none that could surpass those of Justice's own peregrines, of course, which Glasier had caught in the wild and then trained himself for grouse-hawking on his beloved moors.

Martin Leslie first met Irina at Spinningdale and immediately warmed to her. "It was clear that they got-on frightfully well together. They had a lot of common interests, music for a start. And she became a permanent fixture. Which was probably…..well it *was* the best thing that could ever have happened to him. Irina, as she later became, was very, very good for James. There was no way that she was going to put-up with any of his shenanigans."[10]

She had no choice, however, but to put up with some of his old habits, according to friend Roger Upton: "James had a wonderful way of dealing with his post. If a bill arrived he would put it straight in the 'out' tray. When a reminder came he would put that in the 'in' tray and keep the original one in the 'out' tray. And when a third one came along, the original one would be binned. That meant that all of his bills and final reminders etc were kept on strict rotation in his two trays without being paid. I think that Irina used to sort them out when they received a call threatening to cut them off. I also remember that the dining table was always at least a foot deep in un-opened letters."[11]

When Martin Leslie moved to Caithness and had to pass Spinningdale on occasion, Irina and Justice both said, "You must never pass the door, you must come in." This Leslie was only too happy to do, staying for supper before driving home. Sometimes he stayed the night. "And there was the awful occasion when no sooner had I arrived than James said, 'I've taken the cork out of a bottle of really good wine and I've taken the cork out of a bottle of really good port.' So he said, 'I think you'd better stay the night!' I did tell them, though, that I had to be home early the next morning. The three of us had a delicious supper and wonderful wine. Then between us we finished off a bottle of port. It was now well after midnight and Irina said, 'You are impossible. I go to bed. I leave things for breakfast on the kitchen-table for you. I put alarm clock in your room set for 5 o'clock,' and she bid us goodnight. This awful man said to me, 'Come now, are you fit for the second bottle?' And because after you've had a certain amount of port, and are sitting-down, you can conquer the world. So we drank our way through another bottle of port. I have little recollection of what happened next other than actually getting-up a little unsteadily and finding that my undercarriage wasn't working so well anymore. But we got a blow-by-blow account from Irina, the next time we met, where she said, 'Darling, darling….you are so awful the pair of you! You come down the passage; you make so much noise, you bouncing-off the walls. I think you hold each-other up! And when you get to the door into your room you're making so much noise, saying to each other…..giggling like school-boys – 'Shhhhhh, you must not wake Irina!' Irina had been awake for quite a long time!' Oh dear, dear, dear. I had an awful hang-over in the morning going home."[12]

Justice and Irina also took considerable interest in Leslie's choice of girlfriends, who he sometimes took up to Spinningdale. "And then, when Catriona came on the scene and I realised that this could be a full-time arrangement, they were delighted to meet her, and thoroughly approved of one's luck and choice. Unfortunately they couldn't come to the wedding; I think they were abroad somewhere. But they gave Catriona the most wonderful necklace, which became one of her prized possessions. In the fullness of time, when we started breeding, our children were all born in the Dunbar Hospital in Thurso. James and Irina insisted upon coming up to see Catriona when she was in hospital. It caused a great deal of exciement at the Dunbar Hospital when they saw the one and only Sir Lancelot Spratt coming through the door. But it was very, very kind of him to come all that way up and see her."[13]

[1] Torrens, Hugh, *Justice Denied*, Geoscientist Magazine, April 2002

[2] Author interview with Keith Shackleton – 2005

[3] Obituary, Daily Telegraph, 20th October 2001

[4] Daily Telegraph, 14th April 1961

[5] Obituary, Daily Telegraph, 20th October 2001

[6] Ibid

[7] Ibid

[8] Ibid

[9] Ibid

[10] Author interview with Martin Leslie – Isle of Skye – 2007

[11] Author interview with Roger Upton – 2005

[12] Author interview with Martin Leslie – Isle of Skye – 2007

[13] Ibid

CHAPTER 20:
THE FAST LADY

Doctor in Love (1960) was the first of the series not to feature Dirk Bogarde, but the makers felt confident that in James Robertson Justice they had a figurehead for the franchise that the public knew and loved. Just to make sure, they roped in comedy actor Leslie Phillips and matinee heart-throb Michael Craig as new accident-prone doctors, amusingly called (at the time, anyway) Burke and Hare.

Phillips hadn't worked with Justice since they made the Ealing drama *Pool of London*, directed by Basil Dearden in 1950. "I'd seen him around Pinewood from time to time," says Phillips. "In the end, my final count of films made with him was, amazingly, eleven, and he became a great friend. James was in his mid-fifties by then, a great bear with a bushy beard and beetle brows who seemed to scare the pants off most people. As Sir Lancelot, he oozed power and struck fear into all those around him – on and off set. His mere presence was intimidating and a lot of people in the business took him for a loud, bullying bastard, and a nuisance to deal with. I didn't. I found James fascinating and got to know him extremely well. He was a huge personality, a risk-taker and a raconteur who filled the lens of a camera and brought amazing life to the film when playing opposite him. I had to inject him once and, with no help or make-up, his face went bright scarlet – a great piece of acting."[1]

Justice is once again in fine form as Sir Lancelot and gets some fine laughs. Early in the film he announces to his operating staff his impending retirement.

The forever-amorous Leslie Phillips is, as usual, carrying on with one of the nurses. Justice spots him and yells, "And while I still am in charge, oblige me by not fondling my theatre staff's buttocks. Thank you." In another scene Justice is laid low with acute appendicitis and asks one of his old trainee doctors to carry out the operation. The doctor understandably baulks at the suggestion. "Damn it man," roars Justice. "You're being offered the opportunity of slicing up one of the best known bread baskets in Britain. If you don't actually slaughter me you're made for life!"

Justice was never a respecter of convention and thought nothing of wandering around more or less in the nude, according to Betty Box, who recalled that in the operating scene in *Doctor in Love* Justice refused to wear anything under the miniscule hospital robe, which certainly nowhere near covered his enormous bulk. In the scene he had to yell, "Prick me man, don't skewer me. I'm not a shish kebab" at the very nervous anaesthetist. And the camera operator, who necessarily had a ring side seat, said, "Well, from where I'm standing you look like a very generous skewerful of meat." And the whole unit collapsed into laughter, Justice included.[2]

Michael Craig had already made two films with Justice, *Campbell's Kingdom* in 1957 and 1959's *Upstairs and Downstairs*, and found him to be a consummate professional, always on time and courteous to cast and crew. "Although I don't think he was much of an actor, nor did he pretend to be. He always played James Robertson Justice and did a fine line in pompous irascibility, which he varied to irascible pomposity from time to time. He was very good value and I got along with him very well."[3]

The only problem Craig had with Justice, as an actor, was his insistence on the use of real alcohol in scenes that involved drinking. "I remember having to do such a scene with him first thing one morning. He waded in to the real port and brandy and I was obliged to do the same. By the time we finished the scene we'd got through quite a lot of booze and he went home as that was the only scene he had that day. I, on the other hand, had to go on and on through what was a very long day and make the best of my slightly hung-over state."[4]

Like the rest of the series, *Doctor in Love* was made at Pinewood, home of the *Carry Ons* and, in a few years time, the *Bond* movies. "Pinewood was a delightful place to make pictures," recalls Richard Gordon, "resembling a country club with a lively membership in lovely grounds, which I have spotted in many a Rank movie. James was an agreeable and amusing companion in the dining-room or the bar. But he was not a thespian socialite. He preferred to think of himself as a straight forward Scotsman who wore kilts, fished the lochs, flew falcons, lived on The Black Isle, and knew those people over in Balmoral.

LEFT: JRJ as Lord Akenthorpe in the 1961 Miss Marple film 'Murder She Said'. Right: JRJ and Leslie Phillips get to grips with some educational reading matter, in the thoroughly enjoyable 'Doctor in Love', 1960

He continually insisted he was NOT an actor. Perhaps this was affectation. Every performance was himself."[5]

Close friend Jonathan Dalrymple Smith also felt much the same thing about Justice's career. "I'm sure that he never mentioned his film career to me. Of course, he wasn't really an actor; he just played himself. I think he may have admitted that once."[6]

Co-star Leslie Phillips also confessed that he didn't really think of Justice as an actor, "but a great personality. He would have been the first to admit that he could never play a weak or doubtful man, but he was such a powerful and unforgettable character that he filled the screen, and audiences very quickly learned to recognise him. James always downplayed his success as an actor, but I knew that Peter Ustinov, as a director, took him seriously enough, and I thought Betty Box had been inspired to cast him as Sir Lancelot. They both knew what they were doing."[7]

As early as this feature in Picturegoer Magazine, from 19th April 1953, it was acknowledged that the secret to Justice's success on screen was his own larger than life personality that he brought to bear upon his roles: "James Robertson Justice is an actor by profession only; he is not an actor by temperament. This is immediately apparent to anyone who meets him, and should not be surprising to picturegoers. It is the key to his success. What Justice brings to the screen is not acting technique. It is a huge reserve of that rare and powerful thing that I must call character – I would say personality if that word had not come to be associated with mere salesmanship of one kind or another – character as huge as the bulky frame that contains it. On the screen, he directs this force with an intelligence and humour. In a lusty part where he can have full rein, he makes an impact."

Justice always claimed that he wasn't an actor. "He says he's not an actor," Betty Box once ruefully observed. "But he always seems to want an actor's money."[8] Justice also felt that all that star stuff was pure nonsense. At a dinner in Hollywood, Lewis Milestone, who had recently finished directing Justice in *Les Miserables* (1952), said of him, "This is the most extraordinary actor I have ever met in my life. He never wants to be in a scene, he is constantly thinking up ways whereby he can be left out of a scene."[9]

Asked once what he would be if were not a famous actor, Justice replied, "I am not a famous actor. I am a supporting actor who is employed by directors and producers as someone who will turn out a workmanlike performance. I am not a star by definition. I am in this profession to make money and the sooner I can afford to get out of it the better. You can always tell the value of an actor to the box office (although it may not be specifically true it is generally so) by the size of his fan mail. I get 20 letters a year, thank God. I never read them anyway. They go straight into the wastepaper basket!"[10]

However, Justice wasn't immune to turning his fame to his own advantage when necessary. In 1961 Martin Leslie had a brand new Austin Mini van – one of the first produced – and Justice asked for a lift to Inverness where his car was in a garage. "Getting him into such a small van, with seats so close to the ground, afforded all much merriment and James some discomfort although he said he was very comfortable, once in place! Travelling along the five mile straight between Nairn and Inverness, having a heated discussion about something – when in good form James enjoyed a good 'wind-up' – suddenly the bells went and a police car overtook with the sign up ordering me to stop."

A tall policemen got out and marched over to Leslie's window. "Do you know what speed you were going?"

"No," replied Leslie. "I am afraid this mini-van sometimes goes faster than you think"

The policeman straightened himself up to his full height. "You were going 72mph in a 60mph area! Licence and Insurance – step out of the vehicle"

Just then Justice leant over. "I am afraid it is all my fault, Officer, I was having an argument with my young friend, who is giving me a lift to my car, and I may have diverted his attention"

Astonished the policeman sunk to his knees and peered inside. "Is it you?"

Justice stroked his beard. "I am afraid it is"

A look of surprise supplanted the policeman's earlier stern expression. "Doctor Justice, I have seen all your films but never thought to see you face to face." He carried on about this film and that film until Justice could get a word in edgeways when he said that, while he was enjoying the conversation, he was actually in a bit of a hurry. The policeman turned his attention back to Leslie. "I'll let you off with a warning this time – be on your way."

As they drove off Leslie remarked. "Whew – how lucky can you get?"

Wistfully Justice replied. "It does come in handy sometimes!"[11]

As for Justice's general attitude to his profession, it's nowhere better demonstrated than in a conversation he held with girlfriend Molly Parkin: "He said that eventually my life would be far more celebrated than his, long after he was gone and forgotten. Painters, like writers, are in the privileged position of leaving their work behind them, whereas the actor's art is essentially ephemeral by its very nature, the performance over and done with once executed. We argued about this. I cited the cinema to carry my point, that film entraps the performance for all time. But he disagreed, especially when it applied to his own career, which he considered child's play."[12]

Child's play or not he continued to churn out film after film with alarming regularity. *Raising the Wind* (1961) is one of those endearing little British comedies that are so inconsequential but at the same time so full of charm and colloquial pleasure that one can't help but adore them. But there is more than a whiff of *Doctor in the House* about this story of music students and the usual college pranks. Indeed the coincidences are striking, even down to the overbearing but golden-hearted authority figure, played, of course, by Justice.

The film's similarity to the *Doctor* series is no surprise when one learns that Bruce Montgomery, who had written the music for many Box/Thomas productions (including *Doctor in the House*), was the inspiration behind this comedy romp set in a music school. Substitute Sir Lancelot and his three-piece suits for Sir Benjamin, the conductor in a cardigan, and the recipe is almost the same. Base most of the action around a group of music, rather than medical, students and the film almost writes itself. The only problem was the absence of Dirk Bogarde or a comparable star. Michael Craig might have worked better than winsome romantic leading man wannabe Paul Massie, whose main claim to fame was a recent role opposite Tony Hancock in *The Rebel*. Luckily he's backed up with a sterling supporting cast of British comedy treasures – Leslie Phillips, Sid James and Kenneth Williams. Instead of a *Doctor* rip-off, this could also be misconstrued as *Carry on Bassoon*, but with little of the ribaldry or innuendo of that particular series.

Justice, as ever, is terrific value for money reworking his familiar bulldozing persona. An orchestra rehearsal that he conducts in one of the opening sequences is near vintage Justice when he admonishes two students for being late.

The film also afforded Justice the opportunity to display his considerable musical expertise. One afternoon the orchestra's oboe player failed to show up. "Don't worry Pete (Peter Rogers). I can play the oboe," said Justice. He took the instrument and played the Mozart piece with the rest of the orchestra to their satisfaction, and his own.[13] In one of the Doctor films, Justice had to play the bagpipes and Betty Box hired a professional piper and his bagpipes, but Justice insisted on playing the complicated instrument himself. But not before he'd berated the owner for not having greased the pipes with a little treacle, which he said was essential for a good tone.

The fourth, and final, picture that Justice was to appear alongside Gregory Peck was by far their finest together – a stirring adaptation of Alistair MacLean's Boy's Own wartime adventure *The Guns of Navarone* (1961). As Commodore Jensen, Justice has to persuade Peck's professional mountain-climber turned army officer to 'volunteer' for a seeming suicide mission to knock out the eponymous artillery of the film's title. Watching these scenes one can't help thinking what a great 'M' Justice would have been in the *Bond* movies. Throwing a team together at the last minute, matters are complicated when it becomes clear there is a spy amongst them. Besides playing Jensen, Justice also narrates the film's prologue with those unmistakably sonorous tones. Sadly Justice only appears in the film's early scenes, along with another familiar face, that of Richard Harris, the Irish actor and hell-raiser makes one of his early film appearances as a disgruntled Australian airman.

For a film that today is an acknowledged popular classic (there was a time when it seemed almost compulsory to show it on television over Christmas), *The Guns of Navarone* didn't get off to the best of starts when the original director Alexander Mackendrick (best-known for the quirky comedies he directed for Ealing Studios) was fired by producer Carl Foreman due to 'creative differences'. J. Lee Thompson was drafted in at short notice and delivered a fantastic piece of high-class hokum and the top grossing film of 1961.

One of the reasons for the film's enduring appeal is the calibre of the cast. Supporting Peck in his efforts to blast the guns to kingdom come are Anthony Quinn's Greek partisan, David Niven's wonderfully dry explosive expert, Anthony Quayle who gives new meaning to the phrase stiff upper lip heroics and Stanley Baker as a killer who has lost the guts to fight.

Amusingly, Peck never really saw *Navarone* as a straight forward war picture, or so he ribbed the director one day when he explained to him what he thought

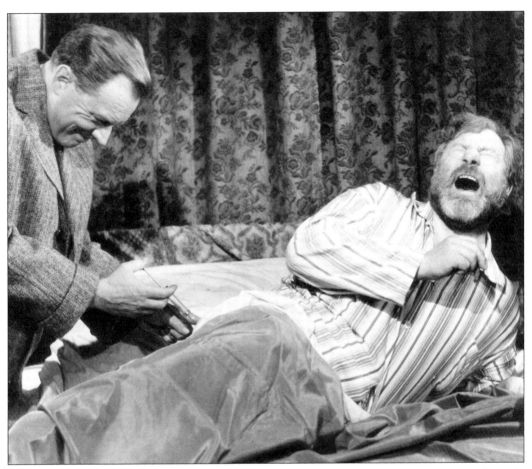

"Don't worry, you won't feel a thing". Arthur Kennedy gives JRJ the works in one of the lighter moments of 'Murder She Said', 1961

the real plot of the picture was. "David Niven really loves Tony Quayle and Gregory Peck loves Anthony Quinn. Tony Quayle breaks a leg and is sent off to hospital. Tony Quinn falls in love with Irene Papas and David Niven and Peck catch each other on the rebound and live happily ever after."[14]

Another of Justice's wonderful screen partnerships was with Margaret Rutherford; they were truly a match made in acting heaven. She had made her name as feisty ladies of a certain age, as had Justice made his name for being big and bellicose. As their personas and acting styles complemented each other so well, it's a surprise that they only appeared in three films together: *Murder She Said* (1961) being the last one, but the most significant for Rutherford, providing her with her most memorable screen character, after Madame Arcati in David Lean's film adaptation of Noel Coward's play *Blithe Spirit*. That role was Miss Jane Marple.

Rutherford had already assayed the role of Christie's female detective on stage and so was the perfect choice to play her on screen in four pictures.

Murder She Said was loosely based on Agatha Christie's 1957 crime novel, '4.50 From Paddington' and to be frank is a bit of a disappointment. When Miss Marple witnesses a murder and informs the authorities, her story is treated with disdain and so she turns private detective. The mystery leads her to the Ackenthorpe household, which serves as a 'Cluedo' board full of eccentric characters for her to suspect. There she gets a job as the world's oldest maid, nursing the head of the family, a domineering invalid, played by Justice. After placing herself in danger, and a couple more murders, the crime is solved.

Stealing every scene that she's in, the indomitable Rutherford makes the role of Miss Marple truly her own, her boundless enthusiasm papering over the film's unlikely plot. Bizarrely, a certain Joan Hickson appears in the supporting cast. Hickson, of course, would later play Miss Marple in a series of highly successful BBC television adaptations.

Justice was once again on familiar ground in *Very Important Person* (1961), a breezy British comedy that poked fun at Colditz-style POW movies. He plays a distinguished radar scientist who takes very badly to life in a Nazi camp. When his fellow prisoners realise he's vital to Britain's war efforts, they reluctantly agree to help him escape. The problem being that his fellow convict comrades are a bunch of British 'silly asses' played by Leslie Phillips, Jeremy Lloyd, Eric Sykes and a new Scottish comedian then making a splash on television – Stanley Baxter.

At the start of the film, Justice is shot down by the Germans, and there is a scene where he has to be stripped and searched, and that involved being totally naked in front of a rather ribald crew. Once all his bits and pieces were off one of the crew said, "Hello James, you haven't got much down below have you". To which Justice replied, "What you cockney fuckers do not appreciate is the coefficient of expansion!" Another member of the crew joined in. "What you mean James is that it's a grower, not a shower!!"[15]

Justice ended up making four films with Stanley Baxter, and the comedian has nothing but happy memories of those days: "I was very fond of James. To me he was just an irascible bear with a heart of gold. Believe it or not I actually appeared on television with James long before I ever met him. I'll explain. James narrated the first programme ever shown on STV (Scottish Television). I was in the show myself, but never got to meet him as he had left the studio before I could say hello. It wasn't until we started filming *Very Important Person* that I actually got to meet and work alongside him. I remember sitting with him on location when a butterfly flew by us. James sat up and said, 'Look, a *Vanessa Atalanta!* I haven't seen one for weeks.' When I asked him what he was talking about he bellowed, 'To the likes of you Baxter, that is what is called a Red Admiral.' James also had the most amazing memory. I once asked him if he actually had what's called a photographic memory. 'I suppose I have,' he replied. 'Except for the fucking lines that I have to learn by tomorrow morning!'"[16]

The clapper-boy on *Very Important Person* was a young chap by the name of Christopher Neame, son of the prolific cinematographer and director, Ronald Neame. Being fairly new to the industry, Neame had been the butt of many a practical joke and it seemed that this particular film was going to be no exception.

"I remember preparing for one particular close-up. I got in to position and was just about to raise the clapper-board when the actor closest to me shouted BOO! – with a kind of honking snarl! I leapt back, dropped my board, and half tripped over an electrical cable. 'Cut!' said the director softly (softly because it was a close-up that was being shot, so there was no need to shout).

Once my composure was recovered and the hoots of laughter from the crew eased, the assistant director got the procedure back up to speed. This time the scene was completed without mishap.

"The cause of this welcome lack of discipline was Jimmy Justice. It was perhaps a bit of an unfair thing to do to an unsuspecting youth like myself, but evidently it was one of his favourite pranks. While still being the lowest of the low (a trainee/observer), I was determined to watch out in case my turn as the victim should ever arise.

"Jimmy's often-seen, choleric screen persona is a great lie – Jimmy was a bear all right, but a teddy bear, who loved his snuff (which he liberally shared with all) and, probably as a result, had a constant twinkle of fun in his eyes.

"There was a degree of rambunctiousness about him, rather like the character of Jock Sinclair in *Tunes of Glory*, played by Alec Guinness on screen and some years before by Jimmy on radio.

"It was hard to believe watching it on the set that day in early 1961.... Jimmy removed his tunic, shirt, shoes, socks, trousers, and shorts.... Then he bent down to touch his toes, thus allowing his fellow actors to perform a convincing inspection! Although it made it to rushes, the footage was never in the final film – it had just been a part of this magnanimous man's sense of on-set fun.

"A year later I was back with Ken at Beaconsfield for *Crooks Anonymous* and, of course, along came all the regular actors. I was again employed as the clapper boy and sure enough, on one of Jimmy Justice's close-ups he pulled the 'Boo!' trick. I was well prepared and didn't flinch. Two weeks later, it was my turn ...

"Another close-up of Jimmy ... 'Sound speed!'

"'Camera speed!'

"I raised the clapper board, turned to Jimmy and shouted 'Boo!' as loud as I could. Thankfully he laughed, but it gave him an awful shock!

"'Cut', said a resigned Ken Annakin."[17]

Justice's next comedy was set in the hallowed halls of the Royal Courts of Justice and its surrounding environs. Another Box/Thomas production, *A Pair of Briefs* (1962) is a slick, if lightweight comedy about recently-qualified barrister Michael Craig who is annoyed when he finds his firm is taking on the boss's niece, played by Mary Peach. The two youngsters soon find themselves in court on opposite sides in a case on the restitution of conjugal rights where both plaintiff and defendant seem to have things to hide.

Justice is perfectly cast as the judge overseeing matters. Bewigged, gowned, and with half-moon spectacles hanging halfway down his nose, he cuts short shrift through the witnesses and barristers alike. Irascible and rather fearsome Justice has little time for the way Craig and Peach seem rather too keen to squabble with each other. Of course this is all a form of foreplay when the warring barristers end up falling in love. Yawn.

Again, like so many of these formulaic British comedies, the gold is in the supporting cast of experienced comic players, like Ron Moody, Graham Stark, Terry Scott, Bill Kerr and Joan Sims. Also, watch out for a great performance from Justice's 'love interest' from *Doctor at Sea*, Brenda de Banzie.

After the delights of *Very Important Person*, the Justice and Baxter bandwagon was soon back on the road with another breezy comedy, again directed by Ken Annakin, *Crooks Anonymous* (1962). Joining Baxter and Justice in this tale about a petty thief joining an organisation for reforming criminals were the usual suspects of Leslie Phillips and Wilfred Hyde White. In the role of Phillips' girlfriend, Annakin cast a young actress who had only just graduated from drama school and was a friend of his daughter's – Julie Christie, destined to become Britain's top female star of the 1960s with films such as *Dr. Zhivago* and *Darling*.

Annakin cast Christie and Justice in his next film too, and recalls how the elder actor was, "absolutely marvellous in his treatment of her in both those movies. His warmth towards her which comes out in those movies is genuine, and shows what a truly great human being he was."[18] By now Annakin had developed a solid working method with Justice. "During the five movies we made together, I would always, having set my unit to work, slip into James' dressing room and discuss what we had to achieve that day. The way I was thinking, and any thoughts he had – and if I thought his idea was a good one, we would kind of play out the scene together, in private (but this was never the way I would work with true or 'Method' actors like Rod Steiger). It was a unique way I worked out of shaping up James – The Natural!"[19]

Justice's stand-in for the film was a chap called William Thomas Wells, (known as Billy 'Bombardier' Wells.) He was a heavyweight boxer and,

Left: From the Roger Vadim film, 'Love on a Pillow', 1962. Right: "Jealous Perhaps?" A pained expression on his face, clean shaven Peter Ustinov tests for quality JRJ's famous beard in London, May 1961. Ustinov had been bearded most of his adult life but needed to be clean shaven for the role of Captain Vere in the film, 'Billy Budd'.

fighting under the name 'Bombardier' Billy Wells, he was British and British Empire Champion from 1911 until 1919. He was also famous for being the second person to fill the role of the 'gongman' – the figure seen striking the gong in the introduction to J. Arthur Rank films. Billy Wells was roughly the same height and shape as Justice, but he was also well into his 70s and not a well man. Incredibly for a stand-in, his feet were bandaged up and the poor chap could barely stand up. In the end the assistant director was forced to stand in for the stand-in![20]

For a self-confessed lover of nature and keen conservationist, Justice was a serious petrol head. His experience on the racetrack proved an asset on *The Fast Lady* (1962), when he drove the eponymous Bentley of the film's title. His pride and joy in real life was a magnificent Rolls Royce that he referred to as *Lady Cab Stanley*. He was once driving past London's Hyde Park Corner, a notorious bottleneck at the bottom of Park Lane, close to Buckingham Palace, when he broke down. This caused a huge tailback. When the driver of a Ford Prefect constantly tooted his horn, Justice saw red and stepped out of *Lady Cab Stanley*, walked over to the offending vehicle, opened its door and said: "If you would like to go forward and fix my car, I will sit here and blow your ruddy horn."[21]

One another occasion he was driving Lady Cab Stanley through Knightsbridge when he knocked a cyclist from the seat of his bicycle. "There was a great commotion," remembers Keith Shackleton, "and James wound down his window and bellowed: 'The devil damn thee black, thou cream-faced loon,' which is of course from Macbeth. James was always quoting Shakespeare and told this story as an indication of how swearing has degenerated since the time of the Bard, because the effect this had on the cyclist was to kill him dead. He just sat on a traffic island looking numb. The point being that if James had called him a bastard or whatever, the chap would simply have stuck up two fingers or something."[22]

But more than cyclists, Justice couldn't abide pedestrians. As he once ranted: "There is nothing as exasperating as a pedestrian who dodders. I would like to see pedestrians controlled by law in the same way that cyclists are controlled. If a cyclist is not showing lights at night he is breaking the law. But a pedestrian can camouflage himself till he is invisible and nobody can do anything about it."[23]

Martin Leslie recalls one particular motoring incident involving Justice. On one trip up to Spinningdale Leslie was without transport and the local garage could only lend him a Ford 7 van. "It was dreadful, well rusted, the brakes were awful (pulling to the left) and they gave me a five gallon can of sump oil, saying I would have to top up the engine every 30 miles or so. I parked it out of the way when I eventually got to Spinningdale and told everyone, James included, that no one else must drive it as it was so dangerous!"

The next day Justice sent Leslie in his old Dormobile to meet some people coming up from the south on the Sleeper train to Inverness. "When I got back, to my horror, I found my van was gone and so was James! He had found the key and taken it to Dornoch despite being told not to as it was so unsafe – he had replied that he could drive anything! I raced to Dornoch expecting to find wreckage on every corner. I found the van outside Grants of Dornoch Butchers Shop with James and his great friend Captain Bob Grant (the owner of the business) leaning upon it laughing and mopping their tears of mirth away. When I got angry about his irresponsibility in taking the van they laughed even louder!"

Justice took Leslie to the driver's side, opened the door, and there was no driver's seat, just a gaping hole with the road beneath it, as far as the foot pedals from the reinforced carrying space behind the seats. Having thought he had mastered the van's little ways, Justice was pushing on down a long stretch of road when he thought he better slow down due to the vibration, the brakes had 'snatched,' he saw a tree coming and had applied his full weight to the brakes – all eighteen and a half stone of it! "The floor had collapsed," recalls Leslie. "His seat went down onto the tarmac, the tree was avoided and his description of trying to hold the van straight, as showers of sparks rained out below him before the van stopped, was hilarious! He then described how he was jammed in the hole and had more and more difficulty in getting out. Luckily there was no traffic and he managed to roll his bulk out onto the road! He pulled the seat out of the hole, its back supporting legs were worn right back to the seat itself, threw it into the back and sat on the load carrying platform. He was able to reach both the steering wheel and the pedals but had to hitch his kilt up off the road before he set off again. His description of his concern for things more important than his kilt being so close to the road as it raced by under him was hysterical, but he said that fear retracted everything and so he was all right in the end! Captain Bob could hardly breathe for laughing and neither could I until James got into his Dormobile, saying he was now late and I would have to get back as best I could! Nowadays it would be a criminal act for a Garage to allow such a vehicle on the road! However, I would have missed an amazing party and a never to be forgotten experience."[24]

The Fast Lady was a sequel of sorts to *Crooks Anonymous*, which although saddled with a formulaic script had managed to turn a modest profit and so Annakin quickly reunited virtually the same team to deliver yet another British comedy of the old school. Stanley Baxter plays an accident-prone cyclist forced off the road one day by a large car belonging to wealthy tycoon Justice. Angry at this display of road rage, the pretty gormless Baxter tracks Justice down to his home and confronts him, only to fall in love with the businessman's eye-catching daughter, Julie Christie. Her passion is fast cars, so Baxter is persuaded by Leslie Phillips' supremely slimy car salesman to invest in a vintage Bentley to impress her – 'The Fast Lady' of the title. The main obstacle is Baxter's lack of a driving licence, but Justice strikes a wager with him: pass his driving test and he may date his daughter. Cue lots of comedic escapades and a crazed – but well co-ordinated – car chase that brings to mind the lunatic frenzy of the Keystone Kops. Annakin also roped in a bunch of top musical hall comics – Fred Emney, Robertson Hare and Frankie Howerd – to play guest spots. Their well-honed skill at getting laughs gave the director a new insight into handling broad comedy that he was later to use with even greater effect in *Those Magnificent Men in their Flying Machines*.

The Fast Lady was shot at Beaconsfield studios, a poor cousin of grander places like Pinewood and Shepperton. Whenever work took him to Beaconsfield, Justice always stayed at the local pub, 'The George', where the landlord gave him the freedom of the place. "He'd wander into the kitchen and raid the fridge when he was hungry," remembered Betty Box. "He soon made himself at home anywhere, palace or pub."[25]

Baxter recalls a strange incident one day on the set of *The Fast Lady* when out of the blue, Justice pulled him to one side and said, "Stanley, I'd rather like you and Leslie to come to my dressing room at lunch tomorrow for a glass of champagne."

"What for?" asked Baxter, "is it your birthday?"

"No," replied Justice.

"A celebration?"

"In a way," Justice went on. "Actually, it's to celebrate the anniversary of me killing my first member of the Wehrmacht".

"Oh! Said Baxter rather nonplussed. "Really?"[26]

Baxter and Leslie Phillips turned up as requested. "I remember he showed us several pictures from his army days," recalls Baxter. "And I remember one particular photograph where he wore a monocle. He looked quite ludicrous but was obviously extremely proud of the photo so I kept my mouth shut."[27]

Another incident stands out in Baxter's mind. They were sitting on the back lot waiting for the start of the big uphill car race, where people had to jump up and down in the car to help it get to the top. There were about 30 cars all waiting for the off and Baxter was sitting right next to Justice in 'The Fast Lady' herself. "Now James was sitting in position with his finger on his temple but was obviously getting quite bored," says Baxter. "He'd been asked to sit like that for continuity purposes, as that was the position he had been in at the end of the last shot, and while the First Assistant was barking out the orders to start the cars, I thought I'd try and break the monotony with a little conversation. God I wish I hadn't!"

"You speak Gaelic, don't you James," said Baxter.

"Yes, I most certainly do," he said.

"Well, I remember one Gaelic phrase my Mother used was 'It's away to plonjoch,' which means that something has gone mushy when it shouldn't have."

"Yes, it certainly has Gaelic roots," said Justice, "but I've never heard of it."

"Never mind," said Baxter, "it's not important."

"But on the other hand it might well be from Barra," Justice continued. "They have quite a few phrases of their own – and I can soon find out because my housekeeper is from Barra."

"At which point," says Baxter. "He leapt out of the car and made his way across the back lot to his dressing room. Now as you can imagine, the First Assistant went crimson and asked James where the hell he was going. 'Mind your own bloody business,' he snapped. The First Assistant looked straight at me and said, 'Where the bloody hell's he going Stan? He's going to balls everything up.' "'I'm not sure,' I said. 'Maybe he's been taken short.' God I was embarrassed. This very expensive scene was being ruined and it was all my fault. Then, after about five minutes (which seemed more like fifty!) he came out of the studio building, walked calmly through twenty two cars, sat down beside me, put his finger up against his temple again and said, 'No, she's never heard of it either.'"[28]

What perhaps struck Baxter more than anything else about Justice was his politics and personal morality. "I think that most people assumed that James would have been a staunch right-winger. You know, one of those old fashioned bigots you get in The House of Lords etc. In fact, they couldn't have been further from the truth. James despised any kind of intolerance, whether it be religious, racial, sexual or whatever. He simply wouldn't stand for it. I've even heard it told that he'd thrown people out of his house for expressing such views."

One afternoon the two men were sitting on the set of *The Fast Lady* having a chat when a member of the crew came and sat with them. This chap had just worked on a film with Dirk Bogarde, who Justice obviously knew well from the *Doctor* films, and for whatever reason he didn't like him. But as opposed to keeping his thoughts about Dirk to himself, he decided to come over and voice them to Justice and Baxter.

"'Ere Jimmy," he started. "You know that horrible fagot Dirk Bogarde don't you? What a nasty piece of work she is." "Well," Baxter recalls. "Before he could go any further James leapt out of his chair and absolutely murdered this fellow, verbally of course. Now, not only was James well over six foot tall, but he also had an enormous temper to match. And I remember that on this occasion he used it to GREAT effect. He said, 'Dirk Bogarde is not only one of the finest actors your country has ever produced but he is also one of my dearest friends. If I ever hear you speak about him again in such a way I will cut off your fucking balls.'"[29]

The Fast Lady proved so popular with home-grown audiences that another Justice, Baxter, and Phillips movie was rushed into production with the actors resuming almost carbon copy roles, but with Peter Graham Scott instead of Ken Annakin behind the lens. Nowhere near as memorable, with its plot about honeymooners agreeing to live with an overbearing father (played by – guess who), *Father Came Too* (1963) is notable for giving Ronnie Barker one of his largest screen roles. Before he died in 2005, Barker was recognised as one of British television's leading comic actors. He was a graduate of repertory theatre and made an early name for himself in radio and then television. Compared to his success on the small screen, Barker's film work was negligible. He played

Friar Tuck in the Sean Connery/Audrey Hepburn historical romance *Robin and Marian* and appeared much later in *My House in Umbria*, but these are notable exceptions. In *Father Came Too* he played the character of a cowboy builder, a role that today can be seen almost as a blueprint for his greatest creation, *Porridge*'s Norman Stanley Fletcher. Barker, however, was no fan of Justice's acting style, or, as he considered it, lack of it. "James Robertson Justice was rather fussy," Barker later recalled. "He insisted on a lot of things being done by a double, like walking down a step. He was standing underneath a beam in the cottage and he said, "I can't do this, my neck's aching.""[30]

Barker would also appear with Justice in the next *Doctor* film, but only in the briefest of scenes. "I had one line and it was shot at Windsor railway station," the comedian recalled. "I came up behind James Robertson Justice. He sneezed, I said, 'That's a nasty cold, you should see a doctor.' He said, 'I am a doctor!' That was it."[31]

Justice is excellent as the father, given to reciting Shakespeare at inopportune moments, and has several scenes of physical comedy, such as when he wakes up the young couple with breakfast, clad in dressing gown and red pyjamas, with a song in his heart that culminates with a short spank on Stanley Baxter's rear! Much of the film, to be fair, is given over to such slapstick, culminating in a finale that includes a fire engine, a herd of cattle and a medieval pageant. Again, no Justice comedy film would be complete without a parade of familiar comic faces, here belonging to Fred Emney, Terry Scott and Peter Jones.

[1]   Phillips, Leslie *'Hello'* (Orion – 2006)

[2]   Box, Betty E.*'Lifting The Lid'* – The Book Guild (2000)

[3]   Letter from Michael Craig to author – 2006

[4]   Ibid

[5]   Letters to author from Richard Gordon – 2005

[6]   Correspondence with author, 24th January 2007

[7]   Phillips, Leslie *'Hello'* (Orion – 2006)

[8]   Box, Betty E.*'Lifting The Lid'* – The Book Guild (2000)

[9]   Picture Post, February 21st 1953

[10]   Ibid

[11]   Author interview with Martin Leslie – Isle of Skye – 2007

[12]   Parkin, Molly *'Moll: Making of Molly Parkin'* (Gollancz – 1994)

[13]   Author interview with Peter Rogers, 2005

[14]   Exact source unknown

[15]   Author interview with Stanley Baxter, 2006

[16]   Ibid

[17] Neame, Christopher *'Principal Characters'* – *Film Players Out of Frame* (The Scarecrow Press, 2005)

[18] Author interview with Ken Annakin, 2006

[19] Ibid

[20] Author interview with Dave Drummond, 2007

[21] Author interview with Keith Shackleton – 2005

[22] Ibid

[23] Radio interview, circa 1960. Programme unknown

[24] Author interview with Martin Leslie – Isle of Skye – 2007

[25] Author interview with Betty Box – Pinewood Studios 1994

[26] Author interview with Stanley Baxter, 2006

[27] Ibid

[28] Ibid

[29] Ibid

[30] McCabe, Bob *'The Authorised Biography of Ronnie Barker'* (BBC Books, 2005)

[31] Ibid

As Sir John, in the 1966 Anglo/German production, 'The Trygon Factor', also starring Stewart Granger and Robert Morley.

CHAPTER 21:
ROUGH JUSTICE FOR USTINOV, CONNERY & MENUHIN

Ever since being elected Rector of Edinburgh University back in 1957, Justice had taken his duties seriously, but his tenure ended in 1960. Elections for Rector were held every three years and on 8 November 1963, to everyone's amazement, he was elected for a second time. His success made history, for this was the first occasion since the Rectorship was instituted at the University in 1859 that anyone had succeeded in becoming Rector again after leaving the post. Both William Ewart Gladstone and Sir Donald Pollock had served twice as Rector, but their terms had run consecutively.

This time, Justice faced fierce competition for the post from fellow showbiz luminaries; old friend and colleague Peter Ustinov, renowned violinist Yehudi Menuhin, as well as local boy Sean Connery. In accordance with tradition, Vice-Chancellor Sir Edward Appleton, Edinburgh University's Principal, announced the result of the poll to a crowd of over five hundred students in the Old Quad from a window of the College's Upper Library.

In all 4,254 votes were cast and the result was as follows:

Dr James Robertson Justice	1916
Mr Peter Ustinov	1521
Dr Julius Nyerere	354
Mr Yehudi Menuhin	239
Mr Sean Connery	224

The announcement was almost lost in a vociferous outburst of cheering and fireworks from the mass of students gathered below who had previously been watching with interest the slow process of clearing the quadrangle of the debris left in the wake of the Rectorial battle which had ebbed and flowed, with all its customary scenes of spectacular violence, during the afternoon. The two main armies were the supporters of Justice and Ustinov, and under the heading, 'Rough Justice for Ustinov,' the Homeric struggle was given eye-witness account in The Scotsman's famous feature, "A Scotsman's Log.' From the account, it was evident that in spite of recent advances in scientific weapons of war, the favourite missiles were still the traditional soot and flour and other less savoury concomitants. Rowdy behaviour was down on previous years, although nearly twenty windows were broken and two casualties admitted to hospital. Both were released on the following Friday, although one student later discovered on re-admittance that he suffered a broken leg rather than just a sprained ankle!

Liberal politician Jo Grimond had been Rector at Edinburgh University from 1960, and was a great success. At the handover ceremony, when Grimond bestowed the Rectorial reins back over to his predecessor, Justice bowed theatrically to the politician and then began his speech: "As I was saying before I was interrupted."[1]

The Student, Edinburgh University's own newspaper, recorded Justice's thoughts at being only the third man in history to have held the position of Rector for a double period of three years: "The exigencies of the trade in which I earn my living… are likely to make my task of appearing in Edinburgh more and more difficult, but I sincerely trust that I shall not fall below the attendance record of my last term of office and that both you and I will enjoy a very happy partnership."[2]

This is indeed what happened as he and Irina's abode became a second home to students and staff for vacations and as a centre for the science departments, including biology and zoology. David Steel, the future leader of the Liberal Party, once ventured there on holiday with another student friend and dabbed for flounders with Justice, equipped with pointed sticks, whilst the actor wielded his old salmon leister.

Justice had been re-elected Rector at Edinburgh University in no small measure because of his enormous success as Sir Lancelot Spratt in the Doctor films, a fact reinforced by the new entry in the seemingly never-ending series, Doctor in Distress (1963), which seemed to revolve around him more than any other character, despite the return of Dirk Bogarde, after a one movie absence.

Top: JRJ chats with two students at the Edinburgh University charities ball during his second term as Rector –
April 1964 (The Scotsman) Above left: Prince Charles with JRJ on a Royal visit to Pinewood Studios in 1962. The
young Prince visited the sets of both Doctor in Distress and Carry on Cabby. Above Right: "Call me Porker!"
JRJ gets ready for an evening out with Leslie Phillips and co in 'Doctor in Clover', 1966.

Bogarde's Simon Sparrow returns for the final time to the corridors of St Swithin's to find his old mentor suffering from a nasty bout of 'love'; the object of his affections being fellow Doctor, Iris, played by Barbara Murray. Asking his former student for advice, Sparrow tells Spratt to lose some weight because he's far too fat. "Fat," blasts Sir Lancelot. "I am not. I am generously proportioned." Spratt eventually looses out to his love-rival, Major French, played by former St. Swithin's student, Donald Huston. After this film, Bogarde jumped ship from the series that had helped launch him to stardom. Four months after the release of *Doctor in Distress*, Joe Losey's avant garde drama *The Servant* opened to rave reviews, totally revolutionising Bogarde's career from matinee idol to serious actor and favourite of the art house set.

The notion of Sir Lancelot falling head over heels in love was an ironic one, since Justice's way with women had become almost legendary. "I knew he was a ladies man," confesses director Ken Annakin, "and occasionally used his dressing room for sessions."[3] Leslie Phillips backs this claim up: "James would let slip when talking about women that he was something of a sexual daredevil. That was his business, but I was surprised by an event a couple of years later, when we were making *Crooks Anonymous* with Ken Annakin at Beaconsfield. I wanted to see James, knocked on his dressing room door and, out of habit, went straight in. There was a young girl with him who jumped up, scarlet-faced. I apologised and went straight out, though James didn't seem particularly embarrassed."[4]

Martin Leslie recalls that there was, "a fairly regular turnover of women," prior to Irina coming into his life. "There was no particular woman for long. Some that you met from year to year, came back. One lady came with her young son. I particularly remember that because I was at veterinary college at the time and James, laughing loudly, said, 'Come here and help, she's got a problem with her son.' I said: 'Good Lord, what am I going to do there?' And he said: 'Well, you'll find he's got a tick upon his private parts and she wants to know how to get rid of it!' It was absolutely hilarious. We went in and there was this poor lad, probably about 10, and he did have a tick attached to the side of his penis. Everybody was slightly worried about him as the bite was just beginning to get a little pink around the edges. It was not the kind of thing you could burn-off with a cigarette-end, although that was much laughed about! We eventually smothered the tick in butter to stop it breathing and eventually it was quietly removed."[5]

As the Sixties started to swing, with the advent of the Beatles, Carnaby Street and all that, the kind of comedies Justice had been making conveyor belt fashion were looking very creaky and old fashioned, especially up against the big

Top: JRJ (as Sir Lancelot Spratt) tries to regain his youthful figure in an attempt to win the heart of Barbara Murray in, 'Doctor in Distress', 1963. Bottom Left: A typical "Spratt" pose, from 'Doctor in Distress'. Bottom Right: "Have at You!" Sir Lancelot prepares to attack. 'Doctor in Distress'.

Hollywood productions that were being made in Britain at the time. Still, he managed to find a role, along with a wealth of other comedy talent, in *You Must be Joking* (1965) directed by a young Michael Winner, who way before his brutal *Death Wish* series, made a number of wacky mod films with a distinct swinging 60's flavour. Shot on over ninety locations and with a script from Alan Hackney, whose main claim to fame was the screenplay for *I'm All Right Jack*, the plot of this energetic nonsense is a simple one. Terry Thomas' army psychiatrist devises an initiative test to discover, "the complete soldier of today." Five volunteers are chosen at random and sent on a mission to pinch, purloin or steal symbols of the British way of life, such as a Silver Lady bonnet emblem from a Rolls-Royce and the Lutine Bell from Lloyds of London.

Winner displays a nice light touch here and a confident way with comedy and comic actors. The film pulls together a formidable cast of British character actors including Denholm Elliott, Lionel Jeffries and Bernard Cribbins, plus Arthur Lowe and Clive Dunn, who would later find fame on one of British television's most popular situation comedies, *Dad's Army*.

Alas, Justice has to make do with a small role as a staid librarian, but he was responsible, so legend has it, for the film's enormous success in Ireland. Suspicion fell on Justice that he had supplied a certain war cry uttered by Lionel Jeffries in the movie. This caused a stir at its Dublin premiere, as far from being a call to arms it was the Gaelic for "Kiss my arse!" and led to it being a smash hit all over the country.

Perhaps suspecting that film work was beginning to dry up, Justice began to diversify and appear more in television. From 18 April to 22 April 1966, he was the storyteller on the long-running BBC children's television show *Jackanory*, reading on each separate occasion a tale from Scotland. His stint on *Jackanory* was repeated but alas it appears the BBC wiped the episodes and they no longer exist. He also turned up in a television special with Lucille Ball called *Lucy in London* (1966); the first occasion America's top TV star had left the US to film a TV special. Justice was but one of a host of special guests, including Buster Keaton, Robert Morley, Peter Wyngarde and pop group the Dave Clark Five.

In the mid 1960's Justice became a regular on the commercials circuit – happily advertising anything from fridges to sherry. Martin Leslie caught the sherry ad one night and was confused. "You see, he hated sherry, and I rang him up and said I couldn't quite believe what I'd just seen. And he had a good laugh down the telephone and said: 'dear boy, I'm being paid in kind. And I'm not cheap.' And I said: 'what do you mean being paid in kind?' And he said: 'Well, I'm getting some of the best wine delivered to Spinningdale.' And in the fullness of time I went down there with Stephen Frank, and James asked us to build racks where his punt-

*"Calm down dear, it's only James Robertson Justice!" JRJ with Michael Winner on the set of 'You Must be Joking!',
1965. (Michael Winner)*

gunning punts used to be, under the garage. The man arrived with a van and we
put the cases of this amazing wine in there. There was Richebourg, Gevery-
Chambertin, Chateau y'Quem, some delicious Port, Chateau Lafitte, and
Margaux. There was wine the like of which I have never seen since. I wished that
I'd kept my wits about me and remembered or written down what we actually
drank from time-to-time thereafter. But, it was brilliant."[6]

Stephen Frank remembers the occasion well too: "It seemed to take us an
age to unload. But when we'd finished I remember James looked over to me
with a huge smile on his face and said "That'll do us for a while Stevie." In truth,
it probably lasted about a week!"[7]

Thank God another *Doctor* film, the sixth, came along to save the day.
Doctor in Clover (1966) had Leslie Phillips wrecking havoc around the hospital
wards. Phillips revelled in the chance to work with Justice again. "I found him

delightful – quite unique, well read and extraordinarily erudite. He spoke ten languages, including Gaelic, and if he told a story he always backed it up with a damned good ending."[8]

The two men also shared an interest in natural gemstones and were having a chat one day when Justice asked: "Do you know anything about jade?"

"Actually," Phillips said, "it's my favourite stone."

"Right!" he declared. "I'll show you a piece of jade the like of which you've never seen. I got it when I was in China just after the war."

The next day, quite casually, Justice came into the studio bar with a stout leather bag over his shoulder. "He put it on the table," Phillips recalled, "and pulled out an object wrapped in a square of black velvet. It was a thick chunk of perfect green jade, about 12x18 inches that must have been worth tens of thousands of pounds. I drooled and stroked it before he popped it back into the bag. He never mentioned it again."[9]

With Bogarde long gone and the series showing unhealthy signs of flagging, *Doctor in Clover* isn't exactly a classic. As usual it's Justice who shines, his eccentric Sir Lancelot Spratt towering over the other cast members and getting most of the best lines: "Could we, by a superhuman effort of will, concentrate on the patients, doctor?" he asks Phillips' bird-mad medic. There are a few priceless gags elsewhere. One arguably the best bit of comic by-play in the entire series. One hypochondriac patient complains of shooting pains down his back and front. "It's my war wound. It's shrapnel on the move."

"And how did it get there?" barks Justice.

"Well, I was bending down in the trenches when suddenly bang, off goes this grenade and a lump of shrapnel hits me right up the..."

"Rectum?" offers Justice.

"Well, it didn't do 'em any good."

For the most part, *Doctor in Clover* plays like a slightly more genial, less rambunctious and considerably less funny cousin to the *Carry On* films, with its sexism from a more innocent age and cavalcade of hit-and-miss old-school gags. At the time the *Carry On* series was at its zenith, with *Carry on Screaming* coming out the same year and *Carry on Doctor* hot on its heels. To be on the safe side, *Carry On* producer Peter Rogers, who also happened to be Betty Box's husband, got Rank's permission to use the word 'Doctor' in his new *Carry On* title. He also kept his wife happy by insisting she receive a percentage of the film's box-office takings. Peter Rogers also included an in-joke dedicated to Betty's Doctor series. Sharp-eyed viewers will spot a portrait of James Robertson Justice in his Sir Lancelot Spratt guise just between the lifts in the hospital foyer. In one scene, Justice's framed portrait stares down from a

Dirk Bogarde checks the pulse of a lovelorn Sir Lancelot in 'Doctor in Distress', 1963.

hospital corridor wall at surgeon Kenneth Williams as he tries to appease angry matron Hattie Jacques with an explanation of why he was caught kissing Nurse Barbara Windsor in his quarters the previous evening. One cannot help wondering what Spratt would have made of them all.

It was on a film set that (indirectly) Justice met Jonathan Dalrymple-Smith, who would become one of his closest friends in the last years of his life. In 1965 Dalrymple-Smith was dating a charming young actress. Unfortunately he was based at Lossiemouth as a pilot (possibly using runways built by JRJ!) and she was in London, so the chance to meet came rarely. One day she rang him up to say that Justice, whom she had met filming, had invited her to stay at Spinningdale. Smith sensed an opportunity to meet the great man but waited until she had been there for a few days before ringing. Unfortunately, she had been delayed and had only just arrived. Here Justice himself takes up the story, as related to Eric Linklater, who had asked how he and Smith had met: "I was filming at Elstree when I met this lovely young thing at the next door table in the canteen. So I asked it if it would like to come and stay. It said yes, so in due course I got it onto the overnight sleeper to Inverness, put it in the car and drove it to Spinningdale. As we walked in the door, the phone rang, and, dammit, it had a boyfriend!"[10]

Three Peregrine Falcons resting on a box cadge in the garden at Spinningdale. (Martin Leslie)

Smith sensed the awkwardness in the situation, but eventually it was arranged that he could come to stay the next weekend. "Which I did," recalls Smith. "Not without some trepidation; James had a fearsome reputation at Lossie as Spinningdale was close to our bombing range at Tain and he frequently rang to complain about the noise. Such was his fierceness and fame that we were threatened with all sorts of horrible things if we ever inadvertently overflew his house. However, he and Irina were charm itself, and I was invited back the following weekend as well. On one of these visits, I think, I first went falconing."[11]

The actress went the way of all girlfriends but, at Irina's insistence, Smith continued to ring from time to time and was always invited to stay. "There often seemed to be falconers there (James himself had no birds of his own by this time), so we were usually out on the hill all day. Irina was a good cook and the food (often the grouse that we'd hawked a few days earlier – James always maintained that a hawked grouse was better by far than a shot one) outstanding. The conversation, of course, was brilliant, led by James. He was

With David Niven and Leslie Caron, in 'Guns of Darkness', 1962

one of those people who, clever themselves, are able to bring out the cleverness in others."[12]

Martin Leslie also talks of Justice's supreme intelligence and breadth of knowledge: "He could argue the socks off anybody, on all manner of things, because he somehow-or-other seemed to know about them. History, science, music, religion, art, you name it and he somehow-or-other absorbed it. He had the most amazing intellectual power which he never put to the effect that a lot of us thought that he was more than capable of.

"James was also very knowledgeable about wine, brandy and malt whiskey. He appreciated such things but never to excess – in my experience anyway. At Spinningdale, on two separate occasions I was present when 'blind' tastings took place. On each occasion someone expert in the field brought with them the wherewithal to test him. The first occasion it was wine – he got the makes right but was out a year or so with one of them. He made no such mistakes with the malt whisky though!

"In addition to this amazing knowledge of so many things – and his ability to go into his library for the relevant 'books of reference' to prove a point – he had this great musical ability already mentioned: Mozarts' horn concerto's on the garden hose, Mozart on the bagpipes, and he played the piano very well. Also, he had a wonderful singing voice of great tone and richness. He could suddenly burst into grand opera (in whatever language was required), often when he was playing it on his sound system. He could also tone it down with great tenderness. His abilities in this respect, when suddenly taking Irina by surprise and singing to her, reduced her to tears on one occasion while I was there, and was of such quality that it put the hairs up on the back of my neck! There is no doubt in my mind that he could have been a great opera singer, if he could have been bothered!"

There is one amusing tale of the time Justice came face to face with Barbara Cartland and the famous author was determined to better the actor. Justice and Leslie attended a party where Miss Cartland was one of the guests. "Barbara Cartland was accustomed to sweeping-into places and taking them by storm, and accustomed to being noticed," says Leslie. "So she came in and found that James, actually, was the fellow who was attracting the most attention. So she made a great mistake, an error of judgement. She breezed-up to James to quietly put him in his place, but found that she'd more than met her match. I think she tried him to begin with on music. James, with his immense knowledge of music, classical music, sorted her out in no time at all. She realised she was getting nowhere with that. So she would try religion. And, although James said he'd had nothing to do with religion, I doubt there was anyone, other than a qualified member of the Kirk, who knew the Bible more thoroughly or better. So she got nowhere with that. Her final throw of the dice was politics. And as he'd stood for a Labour member of Parliament, he knew more about politics and the workings of the Houses of Parliament than she would ever know. And she flounced-out and left the party because things were not going her way. Her departure wasn't really noticed!"[13]

At one dinner at Spinningdale, Dalrymple-Smith mentioned something he'd recently read about; the design of a ring showing men and women having sex in a circle. Of course Justice, the great polymath, immediately quoted chapter and verse and pointed out that it was a design of some antiquity, and dilated on the theme for a while. Irina, getting up to collect plates for the kitchen, said: "Oh, I had a ring like that once."[14]

Justice immediately asked what she'd done with it, since it could be quite valuable. At this point Justice was feeling the pinch – he'd already had to sell his lovely collection of jade.

"Oh, I don't know," said Irina. "I gave it away to one of my innumerable husbands or lovers, I suppose".

Justice glared down the table over his glasses. "What it is to have married a woman with a past."*

Irina, walking behind him with the plates, patted him lightly on the head. "So perhaps at your age you should think of finding someone with a future!" Irina was the one person who could render Justice speechless. He glared at her for a few more seconds, and then a huge grin crept over his face.[15]

"I'm not at all sure why I should have got on as well as I did with James," says Smith. "Certainly, after his strokes, Irina said that he looked forward to my all-too-rare visits and said she thought they did him good. I think we had common interests in the unusual facts of life and history, in music and art, and perhaps we shared a butterfly brain; one subject would trigger off another, possibly very remote from whatever we were discussing. James and I seemed to be able to follow each others leaps and understand what the connection was. Certainly, dinners were punctuated by many visits to the library to look up some fact or another. James had a magnificent sound system at Spinningdale. (Oddly, it was not stereo, which he disapproved of). One afternoon, when there were just the three of us, and Irina was in the kitchen, he said: 'Come on, dear boy, we must conduct some music.' In a drawer he found a collection of conductor's batons. After mulling over them for a moment, he handed me one. 'This should do for you – von Karajan gave me that one.' We put on a Beethoven symphony, loudly, and stood back-to-back in the middle of the room conducting with enthusiasm, punctuated with remarks like – 'Your oboes came in a little late there, dear boy.'"[16]

Over the course of his visits Smith could see that Irina was very much Justice's great love. "He usually spoke to her using the Russian diminutive 'Irinchka.' She was one of the most marvellous characters I have ever met. Very mittel-europäische – think of a slightly moderated Zsa-Zsa Gabor, but with great intelligence. I'm usually very shy, but never felt so with her. She was a marvellous raconteuse; I remember her finishing a story with the triumphant last line, 'So you see, my darlinks, by peeing at the right time, I save the life of my mother!' It wasn't difficult to see what James saw in her."[17]

As time went by, Irina, with typical prescience, bought a property, Tigh-an-Alt, outside Ardgay. It was in ruins, but she set out to make it habitable. "It was slightly unreal," recalls Smith. "To arrive at Spinningdale and have the beautiful, always soignée Irina announce, 'Oh, my darlink, I have just spent all day concreting the kitchen floor.' And she had been, too." As friend Roger Upton recalls, this go-get attitude of Irina was the main difference between the couple:

---

* Justice and Irina weren't actually married at the time

"James and Irina were similar in many ways; none more so than the fact that they were great hosts, great raconteurs and great conversationists. But the main *difference* between them was that whilst James would sit back and *talk* about doing something, Irina would actually go and *do* it. She was a very driven woman and really looked after him."[18]

[1]   McManus, Michael *'Grimond: Towards the Sound of Gunfire'* (Birlin Ltd 2007), p 157

[2]   *The Student* Magazine – November 1963

[3]   Annakin, Ken *'So You Wanna be a Director?'* (Tomahawk Press – 2001), p50

[4]   Phillips, Leslie *'Hello'* (Orion – 2006)

[5]   Author interview with Martin Leslie – Isle of Skye – 2007

[6]   Ibid

[7]   Author interview with Stephen Frank – Birichen Moor – 2007

[8]   Phillips, Leslie *'Hello'* (Orion – 2006)

[9]   Ibid

[10] Correspondence with author, 24th January 2007

[11] Ibid

[12] Author interview with Martin Leslie – Isle of Skye – 2007

[13] Correspondence with author, 24th January 2007

[14] Ibid

[15] Ibid

[16] Ibid

[17] Ibid

CHAPTER 22:
FROM BARDOT TO BANG BANG

Since *Doctor at Sea*, in which Justice had befriended the young Brigitte Bardot, the starlet had become an international sex symbol. In 1962 Justice appeared alongside her in *Love on a Pillow*, a typical piece of art house pretentious nonsense perpetrated by Bardot's husband Roger Vadim. Then in 1967 their paths crossed yet again when Justice was cast in *A Coeur Joie*. This time Bardot played a bored housewife drawn into an extra-marital affair that forces her to choose between husband and lover. Ah, how French. Justice required little assistance with make-up or costume for his role as a kilted laird, a nature-lover using his estates as a sanctuary for birds (and the film's lovers) and his broken-down old castle as a centre for tape-recording bird sounds. Although by now well used to the vagaries of dire scripts, Justice seemed embarrassed, as well he might, when having to apologise to the screen-lovers for his tape equipment being activated during their love-play. His recorders were set off by a certain high-pitched noise emitted by birds, "and it would appear, Madame, that you made exactly the same noise!"

This would be Justice's last screen appearance with Bardot, though the two would star in *Histoires Extraordinaires* (1968) but without sharing any scenes. This quite unique film saw three of Europes's most acclaimed directors, Federico Fellini, Roger Vadim and Louis Malle, adapting three short stories by Edgar Allen Poe. The cast was equally extraordinary – Bardot, Alain Delon, Jane Fonda and Terence Stamp.

With Jane Fonda in the 1968 film, 'Spirits of the Dead'.

Justice next appeared with another stunning French movie actress, Catherine Deneuve in *Mayerling* (1968), a sumptuous historical production shot in location in Vienna. With Omar Sharif and Deneuve as the doomed couple, as well as an all-star international cast and *Bond* director Terence Young this should have been more of a success than it was. On the plus side, it does have Justice whose performance helps bolster an otherwise lacklustre film.

As Edward, Prince of Wales, Justice is perfectly cast as Queen Victoria's heir apparent. From the moment he steps off the train to be greeted by Rudolf, the Emperor's son, played by Sharif, he is clearly on top form. He has to ask Rudolf what national anthem is being played as he complains that he is tone-deaf. Throughout the film, Justice is Rudolf's confidante, as Sharif grapples with his status as ruler-in-waiting. When his love for the beautiful commoner, Maria, played by Deneuve threatens to destroy everything, even Edward is unable to grant him sanctuary.

The rest of the film is a rather stately affair, so Justice is a welcome injection of ribald good humour. Edward's lecherous side is clearly shown, as well as his ennui for state occasions, such as the ballet. At a performance of *Giselle*, he has to ask to be woken up when it is finished, as he knows he will fall asleep. One

Left: With the legendary German soprano Elizabeth Schwartzkopf, after a Gala performance recorded by the BBC in 1967. Right: A rare poster for the altogether bizarre 'Zeta One', 1969. JRJ defiantly did this one for the money.

nice touch is in a hunting scene, where Justice demonstrates his skill with guns. This is also one of the rare occasions that Justice is shown doing anything remotely athletic, when one particular scene takes place on a real tennis court.

From one epic production to another – but *Chitty Chitty Bang Bang* (1968) would prove to be the last film of any merit that Justice ever made. He continued to star in lesser fare for a few more years, but this really was his cinematic swansong. His performance tops and tails this musical comic fantasy that could so easily be mistaken for a Disney film, but was in actual fact a product of the *James Bond* franchise. Adapted from Ian Fleming's children's book by author Roald Dahl, it was brought to the screen by *007* producer Albert R. Broccoli. Another *Bond* connection, of course, was that Justice and Fleming had both worked for the international news agency Reuters in their younger days.

In this classic film, Dick Van Dyke plays eccentric inventor, Caractacus Potts – who lives with his two motherless children – and his equally dotty father, played by Lionel Jeffries. Justice is Lord Scrumptious, the local sweet manufacturer, played with suitable gusto and bluster. As usual Justice gets most of the best lines. When Potts arrives to pitch his latest piece of confectionery Lord Scrumptious gives him barely anytime at all. "Too late," taunts Justice when Potts fails to sell his product. "Had your chance. Muffed it."

Since its original release, aided by innumerable showings on television, *Chitty Chitty Bang Bang* has garnered cult classic status. The blending of reality and fantasy is seamless, with memorable songs provided by the Sherman Brothers – best known for their work on *Mary Poppins*, and ballet dancer turned actor Robert Helpmann's portrayal as the Child Catcher entering the subconscious of generations of children. The film is an absolute treat to watch with a veritable roll call of British film comedy talent from the sixties, Barbara Windsor, Davy Kaye, Stanley Unwin, Richard Wattis, Max Wall, and a rare appearance on the big screen of Benny Hill.

Unfortunatly, Justice's next film and last in a leading role, offers no merit whatsoever. *Zeta One* (1969) is a pretty grotesque affair, mixing soft-core pornography with science-fiction and boasting a screenplay worthy only of the very poorest 1950's B-Movie. The plot (such as it is) involves Zeta (Dawn Addams) who arrives on earth from the planet Angvia (no prizes for guessing what Angvia is an anagram of), complete with a horde of buxom associates intent on taking over the world.

Justice, horribly miscast as Major Bourne, is a (wait for it) sadistic madman, complete with torture dungeon & evil assistant, played by none other than *Carry On* veteran, Charles Hawtery. In what must surely be one of the most bizarre scenes of either actor's career, Justice and Hawtery set about torturing one of Zeta's busty mob (played by a twenty-year-old Carol Hawkins), who eventually dies whilst trying to escape.

God only knows what Justice must have been thinking whilst filming *Zeta One*, but it's certainly a far cry from the relative innocence of the *Doctor* films and is an unfitting end to such a successful and, on occasion illustrious career.

CHAPTER 23:
FAREWELL TO SPRATT
& SPINNINGDALE

Towards the end of 1967 Justice suffered a terrible stroke. "The first I heard about it," recalls Martin Leslie, "Irina told me that he'd got these convulsions and he'd been to hospital to see about it. She said, 'Look, you must come and see him. We're staying in Toby's house outside Edinburgh.' I went in and was quite shocked because of the strength of the convulsion in his right arm, it was uncontrollable and it was all-over the place. The only way he could get peace was to lie on it. So we went through into the private room where there was a very big bed; his weight was considerable, again, almost 19 stone. But he was perfectly lucid and was chatting away about his problem and said it was, 'a bloody nuisance, but don't worry about it.' He said it was going to be OK. He was going to get an operation and they'd sort it and that's what he was down there for. Irina then told me that he'd had the op, he'd come-through it but he hadn't lost his convulsion completely. I remember going down to Spinningdale and seeing him again. He was pretty annoyed that after going through the op the whole thing wasn't fully under control."[1]

The doctors had missed the problem by a fraction. In normal circumstances, they would operate under a local anaesthetic. But because Justice was so large, and because his convulsion was so enormous, they'd had to operate on him under a general anaesthetic and hadn't got it quite right.

"I'm going to go and have another op," Justice said quite cheerfully.

Martin Leslie was understandably concerned. "Is that wise so soon after the last one?"

"They've given me a fifty/fifty chance," said Justice. "Well, I can't live with this and I've had a good life so I'm going to go and have the op. If I don't wake-up well, so be it."

And so Justice went and had the second operation and according to Leslie, "he damn-near died. He was very, very ill." The surgeons had done everything that they could; the procedure had been conducted under local anaesthetic this time, but the shock of two major brain operations over such a short space of time had severely affected Justice and they were quite certain he was going to die. Indeed, the surgeon had given him up, and told Irina, "I'm afraid there is absolutely nothing more we can do for him. What will happen is that he will gently go into a deeper and deeper sleep, which will become a coma and he won't wake-up. And so, we will leave you with him." The surgeons left Irina alone at James' bedside.[2]

An hour later, one of the nurses was coming off-duty and was half-way down the stairs when she thought, I wonder if that woman is still in there with Mr. Justice. She entered the room and saw Irina kneeling on the bed, holding Justice by his nightshirt and shaking him. "No, no, no!" Irina was yelling. "You are not to go to sleep; you must not go to sleep."[3]

The nurse knew that Justice had little chance of making it through the night but muttered to herself, "If she thinks he is worth it then who am I, the nurse, to leave her to do it on her own? I am, after all, the nurse." She bolted out of the room to get her white coat back on and together the two women knelt on that bed and somehow-or-other, between the two of them kept Justice awake until the crisis was past. The nurse later revealed. "I never thought the crisis would pass. I thought he would die. But we finally got him through it, and he survived." As for Irina she never forgot that nurse's intervention. "I remember her, I remember her well. I was deeply grateful to her. She suddenly reappeared and said, "If you think he is worth it, I'll help you!"[4]

Tragically, though, Justice was never quite the same again – never quite 'right.' He did recover, and his friends in the film-world did their level best to try and help him but his short-term memory was shot, he'd always been poor at remembering his lines, now it was just a plain impossibility. A new *Doctor* film was in the works, but in his condition, it was touch and go whether he could even appear. In *Doctor in Trouble* (1970) Justice was to have been offered the best part of any of the *Doctor* films he'd made – two roles in fact, because he was to have appeared as twin brothers – Sir Lancelot Spratt and his twin, Captain George Spratt, commander of a cruise liner. But when Justice turned up at the studio just days before shooting was due to

JRJ and Leslie Phillips take to the wards for the last time, in the seventh and final film of the series, 'Doctor in Trouble', 1970. (Pinewood Studios Archive)

start the filmmakers had to make an awful decision. "We knew that there was no way we could put him through the ordeal of such a heavy assignment,"[5] Betty Box later recalled. "Even though he courageously insisted that he could do it. His hair had grown a little and almost covered the remains of the livid scar on his head. Our hairdresser could deal with that, but although he tried to hide it, he had an uncontrollable tremor in his right arm which would make shooting anything other than close-ups a very tricky proposition."[6]

And so the decision was made to cast Robert Morley in by far the larger of the two roles – that of the ship's captain and Justice eventually got through the few days required for the Sir Lancelot part. "It must have taken every ounce of energy he possessed to do it," recalled Betty Box. "We knew he needed the money and paid him for both parts – he certainly deserved it for long and loyal service."[7]

Doctor in Trouble (in our opinion!) is one of the more enjoyable sequels; its broad humour sailing closer than ever to that of the bawdier *Carry Ons*, but it was not a happy film to make. "We all knew *Doctor in Trouble* was the last movie we'd be able to make with our old friend James Robertson Justice," said Betty. "Robert Morley did all he could to retrieve the comedy for us, but it just didn't work. Situations which would have been hilarious with James were just mildly amusing with Morley, and the whole point of the piece was lost. Leslie Phillips, Irene Handl and Harry Secombe turned in good supporting performances, but the entire project was doomed, I feel, from the day a real-life surgeon said the word 'Scalpel' over dear James's unconscious bulk. What made the situation unbearably ironic was our knowledge that but for the inflated fee demanded by Morley's agent when we were casting *Doctor in the House* 15 years earlier, Morley would quite possibly have been playing Sir Lancelot in the first place. Would the film have had the same success? I doubt it."[8]

Not only did Justice's ill health put pay to his film career but it also signalled the end of the *Doctor* franchise. Although the series would continue on television there could be no more without the actor who had made Sir Lancelot Spratt his own. "Justice appeared in all the *Doctor* films," says Richard Gordon. "But when he died, so did the series."[9]

Watching Justice's minimal appearance in *Doctor in Trouble*, the boisterous, larger than life figure of just a few years before is gone, the verve had deserted him, and he was literally a shadow of his former self. One can even detect his eyes straying off-camera in search of the lines that must have been written on cue cards for him. All very sad, though one must applaud his guts and fortitude for stepping up to the plate and doing it at a time when he was clearly so very ill. Justice was a proud man and he was determined not to let the side down. But one feared that his acting career now was at an end. "His friends got him introducing music programmes,"[10] recalls Leslie. "He read his lines off a prompter, but he'd lost his verve and so that stopped. I remember calling-in one day to Spinningdale on my way north to see him. He never, ever watched television, except for the news and natural history and science programmes. But once this had happened to him Irina told me that he just watched television all the time. When I arrived, Roger Taylor was playing at Wimbledon and he was watching it on the telly. And I said, 'Oh, is that Wimbledon?' as Roger Taylor was just coming off victorious from the court. I said, 'Has he won?' And James said, 'Has who won?' He couldn't remember even though it had only finished five minutes ago. It bothered him, but then he'd forgotten about being bothered, he was onto something else."[11]

"When my son Duncan was born James said, 'When he is 14 I will give him my 20 bore shot gun'. I never expected to hear more of this – but I was wrong. James was back to Spinningdale shortly after his second operation when I called with a 2-year-old Duncan on my way home one day to check with Irina that they were coming to lunch on Sunday.

"We took Duncan into the kitchen to see James' Mynah bird – a great entertainer, it could make noises like an old car starting or an old man coughing, but could also whistle beautifully with great variety of depth and tone. James came into the kitchen and leant on the doorpost. Watching the little boy's enjoyment he suddenly he said, 'I said I would give the boy one of my guns – he must have it now'. He went off to his gun room and came back with his "Cripple-Stopper" – an Ithaca 20 bore pump gun, camouflaged, which he had used when punt gunning. 'I can see by your face it's the wrong gun'. He went off again and returned with his 22 rifle. I told him that it did not matter. Duncan was too young. But he took no notice and returned with his 20 bore. He then insisted on putting it in our car and wouldn't listen to any argument to the contrary.

"I rang Irina that night to say what had happened and that she must take it back after lunch on Sunday as money was scarce and they were going to need to hang on to anything valuable. However, she refused saying that he really wanted the lad to have it and there was to be no argument. It was such a sad moment."

It was heart-breaking for Leslie to experience just how poorly Justice was. "I knew that the wheels were going to come off." When Leslie arrived Irina warned him of what to expect by saying: "Sometimes something happens and we 'lose' him." That's the way she put it. 'The poor darling…you can look in his eyes and see that everything is there, but the link between his eyes and his speech has gone.' She then said, 'You mustn't be surprised if he talks to you in Danish, he can talk to you in French, he can talk to you in German, he can talk to you in Spanish, and he can talk to you in Gaelic. They all come out. You can get six words of one language, five of another and three of another.'" Leslie experienced this one day when he invited Justice and Irina to lunch at his home in Caithness. "I was sitting with him in our sitting-room and he was chatting away about something. All of a sudden, his answers came-out in foreign languages. And he was looking intently at me and I was trying to keep the conversation going. And I managed to keep it going, just by the looks. And he would nod, as if to say, 'You got that right,' but he couldn't communicate. And then I saw….it was like the shutters coming down. The light went-out of his eyes. I knew that he was exhausted by the effort of trying to get it out, and he'd given it up. He couldn't do it anymore. It was one of the most awful moments, because his intelligence was all there but the communication was gone. It got steadily worse. I remember going to see him later and he used to sit in the conservatory of Tigh-an-Alt and watch but he couldn't really carry-on much of a conversation."[12]

It was Irina, of course, who took the brunt of all this, but she coped astonishingly well. Justice would be difficult sometimes to look after because of the state he was in. "Mainly because he was frustrated," says Leslie. "When he got frustrated he got quite angry. I mean, who wouldn't get angry, if you can see everything and understand everything but you can't communicate? You get cross and angry, and Irina was bearing the brunt of all that and doing everything."[13]

It has been hitherto understood that Justice stopped working because he was incapacitated due to ill health. In fact, he went for parts right up until he died, but couldn't take them as the producers couldn't get him insured. One of these roles was Mycroft in Billy Wilder's *The Private Life of Sherlock Holmes* (1970). He was seen along with the likes of Laurence Olivier, George Sanders and Christopher Lee, with Lee eventually winning through.[14]

Already debilitated by several strokes, and with the British film industry in one of its periodic downward spirals, as well as his profligate lifestyle, Justice ran into severe financial difficulties. Then in October 1970 there was this headline from the Daily Telegraph: *Actor Faces Bankruptcy Action*.[15] When Justice's former wife was granted a divorce decree in 1968 on the grounds of his adultery the judge awarded her £50 a week allowance. But payments had recently dried up and Dilys, the ex Mrs. Justice, started bankruptcy proceedings against him in the Court of Session, Edinburgh. Lord Cameron, the vacation judge, issued a warrant calling on Justice to show just cause why his estate should not be sequestrated. He was allowed 14 days to answer the warrant.

In the end, he did not contest the proceedings, was formally declared bankrupt and forced to sell his beloved Spinningdale. As for Birichen Moor, where Justice had spent so many happy hours flying his falcons, it was taken on by his good friend Stephen Frank. Frank had been a farmer in England when he first struck up a friendship with Justice, but it was only when they first hawked grouse in 1963 that they become close. Although Justice must have taken some consolation from the fact that he knew a friend was looking over the property, it must have broken his heart to part with it.

Facing acute hardship, it was their old friend Toby Bromley who came to their aid, allowing Justice and Irina to live quietly in a cottage on his estate in Hampshire. Toby Bromley had gone into his father's shoe business and turned round its fortunes, first in charge of manufacture, design and sale of shoes at Russell & Bromley, latterly, as chairman, where he put on sale the first boots specifically made for women. In 1961 Bromley warned staid British manufacturers: "It's fashion that sells shoes. You must design or die." But, just as the designers of the 1960s were about to follow his advice, he left the industry to become a full-time farmer in Hampshire, and later Scotland, rearing prize herds of cattle, in particular Aberdeen Angus.

Although Justice's ill health virtually forced him to retire from the big screen he continued to work, making two documentaries with Toby Bromley. Originally made by Bromley's own production company, Ashley Manor Productions, the films were sold to Anglia Television to appear as part of their wildlife series, *Survival*. The first of the two films, *The Falcon Gentle* (1974) was filmed by Bromley over eight years using dozens of locations, with the shooting culminating at Spinningdale in 1973. The film starts with a brief history of falconry, starting with its origins in China over 4,000 years ago. It then moves quickly to the 'weathering lawn' (where today's falcons get ready to fly at their prey) and then to a day's grouse-hawking. This section contains amazing sequences of falcons binding to their prey in full flight, or missing them as the grouse jink suddenly upwards. The use of slow-motion in this unique footage enables the viewer to actually see the flying in detail, something that is impossible for the human eye to track at normal speed.

The Falcon Gentle was sold to no less than 53 countries and is still selling in the export television market. Selected by the British Film Institute for permanent preservation (with the master film now stored in the National Film Archive), it was also awarded the Board of Trade's Certificate as being of International Educational Value.

Justice's last appearance on film was in the second of the two documentaries, *The Chalk Stream Trout* (1974) in which he is seen fishing in the River Test, close to his old home in Hampshire. This is a much simpler affair than *The Falcon Gentle*, concentrating mainly on how the River Test is kept pure for fishing, but is certainly no less effective.

No one knows if Justice knew that this would be his last appearance on film but it is fitting that it shows him contented and relaxed, indulging in one of his favourite sports around some of his favourite people.

By now Justice was severely ill. Betty Box recalls, with sadness, the last time she ever saw him alive: "I was at the Connaught Hotel in a meeting with a writer and James wandered in and at first I didn't recognise him at all, poor darling. He didn't live very long after that, and maybe it was better for him to go before he deteriorated further."[16]

His regular co-star Leslie Phillips had also been shocked by the condition of his friend on the set of the last Doctor film. "Sadly, James was too ill to give his usual amazing power; he was in a terrible state. His mind had very little control over his body and he was in a very serious state. Poor James suffered increasing fits and bouts of depression and loneliness, in spite of all the support Irina gave him. It was a shock to see him suffer so much, for he was without doubt one of the most singular men I'd ever met and my memories of him have always remained strong, lasting and affectionate."[17]

On 29 June 1975, practically on his deathbed, Justice finally made an honest woman of Irina, by marrying her. On the wedding certificate, Justice gave his profession as Actor (retired). Just three days later on 2 July 1975, at King's Somborne in Hampshire, Justice died, penniless. A tragic and sad end to a wonderfully, multi-talented man. "My lasting memories of James," said Betty Box, "are his joyful laughter as we had our drinks at the end of the shooting day, the snuff he always used, and the expensive French perfume (often charged to the film!) which wafted each evening from his freshly shampooed hair and his beard, soft as silk."[18]

Martin Leslie made a point after Justice's death to ring Irina once every five or six months, just to see how she was getting-on. She was keeping body and soul together by teaching, mainly Arabs, English as their foreign language. As Irina's knowledge of English, and her use of English, was 'unique' Leslie was sure this would have given Justice enormous enjoyment! When he'd ring and ask how she was coping Leslie always got the same answer: "I am fine darling." And you knew that she wasn't fine, you could tell by the tone. On one particular day she sounded different, this wonderful voice came down the telephone: "Darling, I am so happy!" In fact she was to marry Toby Bromley. His wife, Helen, had died and so these two outstanding people found each other, marrying in 1983 after a short time living together. Then these two remarkable people opened a new, startling chapter in their lives.[19]

Having succeeded as a farmer, Bromley sold his cattle and built a stunning 20-metre, steel-hulled yacht that carried both Irina and himself through polar ice to within 700 miles of the North Pole, and later up the Orinoco River in South America. Together they covered more than 35,000 miles of ocean, and the experience turned both into passionate conservationists. "They had wonderful times, and it was really brilliant," says Leslie. "They were very happy together and complemented each other so well."

After they had returned from the Arctic, Leslie paid the couple a visit when he was in the south. "They were full of welcome and she said, 'Darling, we have something that we acquired on our travels and have kept the last of it especially for you, we have muk-tuk.' Muk-tuk turned-out to be diced narwhal blubber, which is meant to be a delicacy! It's terribly chewy. It's got an interesting taste but its consistency is not very conducive to anything much! Anyway, you dutifully chewed away and finally got through it. Then I got taken in to supper and she said, 'We also keep for you darling, the last of the narwhal itself. You have narwhal stew; you've never had narwhal stew!' Never had I had narwhal stew and if I was ever offered narwhal stew again I would be off, out of that building running! Because, at about 1 o'clock in the morning the combination of the blubber and the stew got to me and I have seldom been so ill. It poisoned my system!"[20]

Irina and Toby Bromley were certainly a unique couple, often spotted bombing around the English countryside in an open-topped sports car, even when their combined ages were one hundred and seventy-five. It suited their mutually exuberant appetite for living. At the age of 80 Bromley sold his boat and converted his wildfowl collection into a natural habitat for British water birds. At the same time, he began to create Wyld Court Rainforest in Berkshire, a 20,000 sq ft climate-controlled area under glass in which three different kinds of rainforest grew, conserving rare plants as well as animal species such as the golden tamarin monkey. Completed in 1993, this was later given to a conservation charity, leaving Bromley free to devote his energies to what he termed, "the most important work of my life," the creation of the Bromley Trust.

Sadly, in 2001 Irina passed away aged 85. Bromley continued his charity work until his own death in 2003 aged 91. He was survived by a son, Roderick, from his first marriage.

Although a memorial service was held for James Robertson Justice at Winchester Cathedral, organised personally by Irina featuring all the music she knew he loved, perhaps the most fitting tribute to him came on 11 August 1975, when Irina and a party of his friends, attended a ceremony on the moor where Justice had hawked for many years. Out of the blue, Martin Leslie got a phone call from Irina. "Can you come? We're going to put James' ashes in his favourite falconry bag and take it up onto Birichen Moor."??

Everybody met up; Irina was there, of course, along with Stephen Frank and Roger Upton. "We all tried to make it as happy an occasion as possible really," says Stephen. Fittingly a cairn had been constructed and with a piper in full dress and falconers with hooded falcons on their fists. The ashes of James Robertson Justice were interred within, enclosed inside with his favourite hawking-bag. A bottle of his preferred tipple, Talisker whisky from the Isle of Skye, accompanied his last remains.

The cairn still stands there today; a fitting monument to a life lived in a way that all lives should be led – to the fullest. Justice would also have enjoyed the recent increase of birds of prey in the Spinningdale area. Local resident, Charlie Miller has recently seen ospreys, herons, peregrine falcons and even a red kite. Buzzards are nearly as common as sparrows now. Also in the area, out on the moors there are reports of young golden eagle hunting, and at the opposite end of the raptor scale, merlins!

Without his film career, Justice would probably have been another loveable British eccentric, one of those blithe spirits that flitter in and out of life, illuminating the lives of others. Smothered by political correctness and socio-political paranoia, he reminds us of a world that appeared simpler, if only on the surface.

James Robertson Justice's screen character was like a giant panda – cuddly to look at but peppery within. The crinkly, benign eyes could suddenly turn very nasty indeed. But when he was jolly he was everyone's favourite uncle, and when he chortled it rumbled and shook his 250-pound frame like the onset of an earthquake.

Justice was a canny Scot who refused to take either himself or the trade he practised seriously. He described himself as a terrible actor with no right whatever to stardom, and remained genuinely mystified by the eagerness of producers to pay him, by his reckoning, astronomical sums simply to go before the cameras and be himself. "If the public wish to see that, that's their affair," he would growl if quizzed on the subject of his film stardom. "I'm an intelligent layman rather than an actor."

So, was he a character actor? Or merely a character who acted? That will always be open for debate. However, the fact that his film career lasted for over a quarter of a century – and featured roles in a handful of truly classic movies is without doubt a testament to his ability.

[1] Author interview with Martin Leslie – Isle of Skye – 2007

[2] Ibid

[3] Ibid

[4] Ibid

[5] Author interview with Betty E Box – Pinewood Studios – July 1994

[6] Ibid

[7] Ibid

[8] Ibid

[9] Letters to author from Richard Gordon – 2005

[10] Author interview with Martin Leslie – Isle of Skye – 2007

[11] Ibid

[12] Ibid

[13] Ibid

[14] Chandler, Charlotte 'Nobody's Perfect: Billy Wilder – A Personal Biography'
     (Pocket Books – 2003) p 257

[15] Daily Telegraph, 28th October, 1970

[16] Author interview with Betty E Box – Pinewood Studios – July 1994

[17] Phillips, Leslie 'Hello' (Orion – 2006)

[18] Author interview with Betty E Box – Pinewood Studios – July 1994

[19] Author interview with Martin Leslie – Isle of Skye – 2007

[20] Author interview with Martin Leslie – Isle of Skye – 2007

AFTERWORD

Using so many contributions from people who knew and worked with James Robertson Justice, Mr. Hogg has produced a fascinating and very true story of a Scotsman who was one of cinema's most unique and very fascinating characters.

James Robertson Justice wasn't at all a typical Actor. Because of his many unusual real life experiences, James was able to bring much more to any role than the Screenwriter had envisioned, and this made him a real gift for any Director.

I loved working with him – he always added something unexpectedly which furthered the character he was portraying, and I believe James deserves his place in my gallery of great British, American and French movie stars that I have worked with, and this book is a fine tribute!.

Ken Annakin
Beverly Hills, California
January 2008

FILMOGRAPHY

Feature Films

FOR THOSE IN PERIL (1944)
GB. 77 minutes. Black and White
Ealing
Director: Charles Crichton
Screenplay: T.E.B Clark, J.O.C Orton, Harry Watt,
Richard Hillary (story)
Cast: David Farrar, Peter Arne, Anthony Bushell
JRJ: Operations Room Officer (uncredited)

CHAMPAGNE CHARLIE (1944)
GB. 105 minutes. Black and White
Ealing
Director: Harry Watt
Screenplay: Angus McPhail, Diana Morgan, Harry Watt
Cast: Tommy Trinder, Stanley Holloway, Betty Warren,
Jean Kent
JRJ: Centurion

FIDDLERS THREE (1944)
GB. 88 minutes. Black and White
Ealing
Director: Alberto Cavalcanti
Screenplay: John Dighton, Angus McPhail, Austin
Melford
Cast: Tommy Trinder, Frances Day, Sonnie Hale, Francis
L Sullivan
JRJ: Patron

APPOINTMENT WITH CRIME (1946)
GB. 90 minutes. Black and White
British National
Director: John Harlow
Screenplay: John Harlow, Michael W Leighton (story)
Cast: William Hartnell, Robert Beatty, Joyce Howard,
Herbert Lom

HUNGRY HILL (1947)
GB. 92 minutes. Black and White
GFD/Two Cities
Director: Brian Desmond Hurst
Screenplay: Terence Young, Francis Crowdy, Daphne Du
Maurier (novel)
Cast: Margaret Lockwood, Dennis Price, Cecil Parker,
Dermot Walsh, Michael Denison

AGAINST THE WIND (1948)
GB. 96 minutes. Black and White
Ealing
Director: Charles Crichton
Screenplay: T.E.B Clarke, Michael Pertwee, J Elder Willis
(story)
Cast: Robert Beatty, Simone Signoret, Jack Warner,
Gordon Jackson, Paul Dupuis
JRJ: Akerman

VICE VERSA (1948)
GB. 111 minutes. Black and White
Rank/Two Cities
Director: Peter Ustinov
Screenplay: Peter Ustinov, F Anstey (novel)
Cast: Roger Livesey, Kay Walsh, Petula Clark, JRJ, David
Hutcheson, Anthony Newley
JRJ: Dr Grimstone

SCOTT OF THE ANTARCTIC (1948)
GB. 111 minutes. Colour
Ealing
Director: Charles Frend
Screenplay: Walter Meade, Ivor Montagu, Mary Hayley
Bell (additional dialogue)
Cast: John Mills, Diana Churchill, Harold Warrender,
JRJ, Anne Firth, Derek Bond, Reginald Beckwith
JRJ: Taff Evans

MY BROTHER JONATHAN (1948)
GB. 102 minutes. Colour
ABP
Director: Harold French
Screenplay: Adrian Alington, Leslie Landau, Francis Brett
Young (novel)
Cast: Michael Denison, Dulcie Gray, Stephen Murray,
Ronald Howard, Mary Clare
JRJ: Eugene Dakers

QUARTET (1948)
GB. 120 minutes. Colour
Gainsborough/J Arthur Rank Films
Directors: Ken Annakin, Harold French, Ralph Smart,
Arthur Crabtree
Screenplay: W Somerst Maugham, R C Sherriff
Cast: Cecil Parker, Ernest Thesiger, Wilfred Hyde White,
Linden Travers, Mai Zetterling, Nora Swinburne, Felix
Aylmer, Henry Edwards
JRJ: Branksome

WHISKY GALORE! (1949)
aka Tight Little Island (USA)
GB. 82 minutes. Black and White
Ealing
Director: Alexander Mackendrick
Screenplay: Angus McPhail, Compton MacKenzie
Cast: Basil Radford, Catherine Lacey, Bruce Seton, JRJ,
Joan Greenwood, Wylie Watson, Gordon Jackson, John
Gregson
JRJ: Dr Maclaren

CHRISTOPHER COLUMBUS (1949)
GB. 104 minutes. Colour
Rank/Gainsborough
Director: David MacDonald
Screenplay: Muriel Box, Sydney Box, Cyril Roberts,
Rafael Sabatini (novel)
Cast: Fredric March, Florence Eldridge, Francis L
Sullivan, Kathleen Ryan, Derek Bond
JRJ: Martin Pinzon

STOP PRESS GIRL (1949)
GB. 78 minutes. Black and White/Colour
Rank
Director: Michael Barry
Screenplay: T J Morrison (also story), Basil Thomas
(story)
Cast: Sally Anne Howes, Gordon Jackson, Basil Radford,
Naunton Wayne
JRJ: Mr. Peters

PRIVATE ANGELO (1949)
GB. 106 minutes. Black and White
Pilgrim
Directors: Michael Anderson, Peter Ustinov
Screenplay: Michael Anderson, Peter Ustinov, Eric
Linklater (novel)
Cast: Godfrey Tearle, María Denis, Peter Ustinov,
Marjorie Dennis, Robin Bailey
JRJ: Feste

POET'S PUB (1949)
GB. 79 minutes. Black and White
GFD/Aquila
Director: Frederick Wilson
Screenplay: Diana Morgan, Eric Linklater (novel)
Cast: Derek Bond, Rona Anderson, John McLaren,
Barbara Murray, Joyce Grenfell
JRJ: Prof. Benbow

MY DAUGHTER JOY (1950)
aka Operation X (USA)
US. 81 minutes. Black and White
Director: Gregory Ratoff
Screenplay: William Rose, Robert Thoeren, Irene
Nemirowsky (novel "David Golder")
Cast: Edward G Robinson, Peggy Cummins, Richard
Greene, Nora Swinburne, Walter Rilla, Finlay Currie
JRJ: Prof. Keval

THE BLACK ROSE (1950)
GB. 120 minutes. Colour
Twentieth Century Fox
Director: Henry Hathaway
Screenplay: Talbot Jennings, Thomas B Costain (novel)
Cast: Tyrone Power, Orson Welles, Cécile Aubry, Jack
Hawkins, Michael Rennie, Finlay Currie, Herbert Lom
JRJ: Simeon Beutrie

PRELUDE TO FAME (1950)
GB. 88 minutes. Black and White
Rank/Two Cities
Director: Fergus McDonnell
Screenplay: Robert Westerby, Bridgit Boland (additional
dialogue)
Cast: Guy Rolfe, Kathleen Byron, Kathleen Ryan, Jeremy
Spenser, Henry Oscar
JRJ: Sir Arthur Harold

THE MAGNET (1950)
GB. 79 minutes. Black and White
Ealing
Director: Charles Frend
Screenplay: T E B Clarke
Cast: Stephen Murray, Kay Walsh, James Fox, Meredith
Edwards, Thora Hird
JRJ (as Seamus Mor na Feaseg): Tramp

BLACKMAILED (1950)
GB. Black and White
GFD/Harold Huth
Director: Marc Allegret
Screenplay: Hugh Mills, Roger Vadim, Elizabeth Myers
(novel "Mr Christopher")
Cast: Mai Zetterling, Dirk Bogarde, Fay Compton,
Robert Flemyng, Michael Gough
JRJ: Mr Sine

POOL OF LONDON (1951)
GB. 85 minutes. Black and White
Ealing
Director: Basil Dearden
Screenplay: John Eldridge, Jack Whittingham
Cast: Bonar Colleano, Earl Cameron, Susan Shaw, Renée
Anderson, Moira Lister, Max Adrian
JRJ: Engine Room Officer Trotter

CAPTAIN HORATIO HORNBLOWER R N (1951)
aka Captain Horatio Hornblower (USA)
GB/US. 117 minutes. Colour
Warner
Director: Raoul Walsh
Screenplay: Ivan Goff, Ben Roberts, Aeneas Mackenzie,
C S Forester (novel & adaptation)
Cast: Gregory Peck, Virginia Mayo, Robert Beatty,
Moultrie Kelsall, Terence Morgan, James Kenney
JRJ (as James R. Justice): Seaman Quist

DAVID AND BATHSHEBA (1951)
US. 116 minutes. Colour
Twentieth Century Fox
Director: Henry King
Screenplay: Philip Dunne
Cast: Gregory Peck, Susan Hayward, Raymond Burr,
Kieron Moore
JRJ: Abishai

ANNE OF THE INDIES (1951)
US. 81 minutes. Colour
Twentieth Century Fox
Director: Jacques Tourneur
Screenplay: Arthur Caesar, Philip Dunne, Herbert
Ravenel Sass (story)
Cast: Jean Peters, Louis Jourdan, Debra Paget, Herbert
Marshall
JRJ: Red Dougal

THE LADY SAYS NO! (1952)
US. 80 minutes. Black and White
United Artists
Director: Frank Ross
Screenplay: Robert Russell
Cast: Joan Caufield, David Niven, Lenore Lonergan,
Frances Bavier
JRJ: Matthew Hatch

THE STORY OF ROBIN HOOD AND HIS
MERRIE MEN (1952)
aka The Story of Robin Hood (USA)
USA. 84 minutes. Colour
Walt Disney
Director: Ken Annakin
Screenplay: Lawrence Edward Watkin
Cast: Richard Todd, Peter Finch, Michael Hordern, Bill
Owen, Bill Travers, James Hayter, Martita Hunt, Joan
Rice
JRJ: Little John

LES MISERABLES (1952)
US 106. minutes. Black and White
Twentieth Century Fox
Director: Lewis Milestone
Screenplay: Richard Murphy, Victor Hugo
Cast: Michael Rennie, Debra Paget, Edmund Gwenn,
Cameron Mitchell, Sylvia Sidney, Elsa Lanchester
JRJ: Robert

THE VOICE OF MERRILL (1952)
aka Murder Will Out (US)
GB. 84 minutes. Black and White
Tempean
Director: John Gilling
Screenplay: John Gilling, Gerald Landeau (story),
Terence Austin (story)
Cast: Valerie Hobson, Edward Underdown, Henry
Kendall, Garry Marsh, Sam Kydd
JRJ: Jonathan

MISS ROBIN HOOD (1952)
GB. 76 minutes. Black and White
Group 3
Director: John Guillermin
Screenplay: Patrick Campbell, Val Valentine, Reed de
Rouen (story)
Cast: Margaret Rutherford, Richard Hearne, Dora Bryan,
Michael Medwin, Sid James, Kenneth Connor
JRJ: The Macalister

THE SWORD AND THE ROSE (1953)
aka When Knighthood Was In Flower (US) TV Title
US. 92 minutes. Colour
Walt Disney
Director: Ken Annakin
Screenplay: Lawrence Edward Watkin, Charles Major
(novel)
Cast: Richard Todd, Glynis Johns, Michael Gough, Peter
Copley, Jane Barrett
JRJ: King Henry VIII

ROB ROY, THE HIGHLAND ROGUE (1954)
GB. 81 minutes. Colour
Walt Disney
Director: Harold French
Screenplay: Lawrence Edward Watkin, Sir Walter Scott
(novel)
Cast: Richard Todd, Glynis Johns, Michael Gough, Finlay
Currie,
JRJ: Duke of Argyll

DOCTOR IN THE HOUSE (1954)
GB. 91 minutes. Colour
Rank
Director: Ralph Thomas
Screenplay: Nicholas Phipps, Richard Gordon (novel and
adaptation)
Cast: Dirk Bogarde, Kenneth More, Donald Sinden,
Donald Houston, Kay Kendall, Muriel Pavlow, Geoffrey
Keen
JRJ: Sir Lancelot Spratt

OUT OF THE CLOUDS (1955)
GB. 88 minutes. Colour
Ealing
Director: Basil Dearden
Screenplay: John Eldridge, Michael Relph, Rex Reinits
(adaptation), John Fores (novel "The Springboard")
Cast: Anthony Steel, Robert Beatty, David Knight,
Margo Lorenz, Bernard Lee, Esma Cannon, Sid James
JRJ: Captain Brent

LAND OF THE PHAROAHS (1955)
USA. 105 minutes. Colour
Warner
Director: Howard Hawks
Screenplay: Harold Jack Bloom, William Faulkner, Harry Kurnitz
Cast: Jack Hawkins, Joan Collins, Denny Martin, Alexis Minotis, Luisella Boni, Sydney Chaplin, James Hayter
JRJ: Vashtar

ABOVE US THE WAVES (1955)
GB. 99 minutes. Black and White
Rank
Director: Ralph Thomas
Screenplay: Robin Estridge
Cast: John Mills, John Gregson, Donald Sinden, Michael Medwin, James Kenney, Anthony Newley
JRJ: Admiral Ryder

STORM OVER THE NILE (1955)
GB. 107 minutes. Colour
London Film Productions
Director: Zoltan Korda, Terence Young
Screenplay: R C Sherriff, A E W Mason (novel "The Four Feathers")
Cast: Anthony Steel, Laurence Harvey, Mary Ure, Geoffrey Keen, Michael Hordern, Ian Carmichael, Christopher Lee
JRJ: General Burroughs

DOCTOR AT SEA (1955)
GB. 93 minutes. Colour
Rank
Director: Ralph Thomas
Screenplay: Nicholas Phipps, Jack Davies, Richard Gordon (novel)
Cast: Dirk Bogarde, Brigitte Bardot, Brenda de Banzie, Maurice Denham, Michael Medwin, Raymond Huntley, Geoffrey Keen
JRJ: Captain Hogg

AN ALLIGATOR CALLED DAISY (1955)
GB. 88 minutes. Colour
Rank
Director: J Lee-Thompson
Screenplay: Jack Davies, Charles Terrott (novel)
Cast: Donald Sinden, Jeannie Carson, Diana Dors, Roland Culver, Stanley Holloway, Richard Wattis
JRJ: Sir James Colebrook

MOBY DICK (1956)
aka Herman Melville's Moby Dick (USA)
GB. 115 minutes. Colour
Moulin/Warner
Director: John Huston
Screenplay: Ray Bradbury, John Huston, Herman Melville (novel)
Cast: Gregory Peck, Richard Basehart, Leo Genn, Harry Andrews, Bernard Miles, Noel Purcell, Mervyn Johns, Joseph Tomelty, Francis De Wolff
JRJ: Captain Boomer

THE IRON PETTICOAT (1956)
GB. 96 minutes. Colour
MGM
Director: Ralph Thomas
Screenplay: Ben Hecht, Harry Saltzman (story)
Cast: Bob Hope, Katherine Hepburn, Robert Helpmann, David Kossoff
JRJ: Colonel Sklarnoff

CHECKPOINT (1956)
GB. 86 minutes. Colour
Rank
Director: Ralph Thomas
Screenplay: Robin Estridge
Cast: Anthony Steel, Odile Versois, Stanley Baker, Maurice Denham, Michael Medwin
JRJ: Warren Ingram

THE LIVING IDOL (1957)
US/Mexico. 100 minutes. Colour
MGM
Director: Rene Cardona, Albert Lewin
Screenplay: Albert Lewin
Cast: Steve Forrest, Liliane Montevecchi, Sara García, Eduardo Noriega
JRJ: Doctor Alfred Stoner

DOCTOR AT LARGE (1957)
GB. 98 minutes. Colour
Rank
Director: Ralph Thomas
Screenplay: Nicholas Phipps, Richard Gordon (novel)
Cast: Dirk Bogarde, Muriel Pavlow, Donald Sinden, Shirley Eaton, Michael Medwin, Lionel Jeffries
JRJ: Sir Lancelot Spratt

SOUVENIR D'ITALIE (1957)
aka It Happened in Rome (USA)
Italy/GB. 100 minutes. Colour
Director:
Screenplay: Antonio Pietrangeli, Dario Fo, Furio Scarpelli, Agenore Incrocci
Cast: June Laverick, Isobel Corey, Ingebord Schöner, Gabrielle Ferzetti

SEVEN THUNDERS (1957)
aka The Beasts of Marsellies (USA)
GB. 100 minutes. Black and White
Rank
Director: Hugo Fregonese
Screenplay: John Baines, Rupert Croft-Cooke (novel)
Cast: Stephen Boyd, Kathleen Harrison, Tony Wright, Anna Gaylor, Rosalie Crutchley, Anton Diffring
JRJ: Dr Martout

CAMPBELL'S KINGDOM (1957)
GB. 102 minutes. Colour
Rank
Director: Ralph Thomas
Screenplay: Robin Estridge, Hammond Innes (also novel)
Cast: Dirk Bogarde, Stanley Baker, Michael Craig, Barbara Murray, Sid James
JRJ: James MacDonald

THÉRÈSE ÉTIENNE (1958)
France/Italy. 90 minutes. Black and White
Director: Denys de la Patellier
Screenplay: Denys de la Patellier, Roland Laudenbach, John Knittel (novel)
Cast: Francoise Arnoul, René Berthier, Roger Burckhardt, Georges Chamarat
JRJ: Anton Muller

ORDERS TO KILL (1958)
GB. 111 minutes. Black and White
Director: Anthony Asquith
Screenplay: George St George, Paul Dehn, Donald Downes (novel)
Cast: Paul Massie, Irene Worth, Leslie French, Eddie Albert, Lillian Gish, John Crawford, Lionel Jeffries
JRJ: Naval Commander

UPSTAIRS AND DOWNSTAIRS (1959)
GB. 101 minutes. Colour
Rank
Director: Ralph Thomas
Screenplay: Frank Harvey, Ronald Scott-Thorn (novel)
Cast: Michael Craig, Anne Heywood, Mylène Demongeot, Claudia Cardinale, Sid James, Joan Sims, Joan Hickson, Joseph Tomelty
JRJ: Mansfield

DIE BOTSCHAFTERIN (1960)
West Germany. 114 minutes. Black and White
Filmaufbau/NF
Director: Harald Braun
Screenplay: Rolf Thiele, Harald Braun, Hans Wolfgang (novel)
Cast: Nadja Tiller, Hansjörg Felmy, Irene von Meyendorff, Günther Schramm
JRJ: Robert Morrison

DOCTOR IN LOVE (1960)
GB. 93 minutes. Colour
Rank
Director: Ralph Thomas
Screenplay: Nicholas Phipps, Richard Gordon (novel)
Cast: Michael Craig, Leslie Phillips, Virginia Maskell, Carole Lesley, Joan Sims
JRJ: Sir Lancelot Spratt

A FRENCH MISTRESS (1960)
GB. 94 minutes. Black and White
British Lion/Charter
Director: Roy Boulting
Screenplay: Roy Boulting, Robert Monroe (play)
Cast: Ian Bannen, Robert Bruce, Jeremy Bulloch, Denise Coffey, Michael Crawford
JRJ: Robert Martin – AKA Bow Wow

FOXHOLE IN CAIRO (1961)
GB. 80 minutes. Black and White
Omnia
Director: John Llewellyn-Moxey
Screenplay: Donald Taylor, Leonard Mosley (also novel "The Cat and the Mice")
Cast: Adrian Hoven, Niall MacGinnis, Peter van Eyck, Robert Urquhart, Neil McCallum, Fenella Fielding
JRJ: Captain Robertson

THE GUNS OF NAVARONE (1961)
USA/Yugoslavia. 158 minutes. Colour
Columbia
Director: J Lee-Thompson
Screenplay: Carl Foreman, Alistair MacLean (novel)
Cast: Gregory Peck, David Niven, Anthony Quinn, Stanley Baker, Anthony Quayle, James Darren, Irene Papas, Gia Scala
JRJ: Prologue Narrator & Commodore Jensen

VERY IMPORTANT PERSON (1961)
aka A Coming Out Party (US)
GB. 98 minutes. Black and White
Rank/Independent Artists
Director: Ken Annakin
Screenplay: Henry Blyth, Jack Davies, John Foley (novel – uncredited)
Cast: Stanley Baxter, Leslie Phillips, Eric Sykes, Richard Wattis, Colin Gordon
JRJ: Sir Earnest Pease & Lt. Farrow

RAISING THE WIND (1961)
GB. 91 minutes. Colour
Anglo Amalgamated
Director: Gerald Thomas
Screenplay: Bruce Montgomery
Cast: Leslie Phillips, Paul Massie, Kenneth Williams, Liz Fraser, Eric Barker, Jennifer Jayne, Jim Dale
JRJ: Sir Benjamin Boyd

MURDER SHE SAID (1961)
Aka Agatha Christie's 'Murder She Said'
GB. 87 minutes. Black and White
MGM
Director: George Pollock
Screenplay: David Pursall, Jack Seddon, Agatha Christie
(novel "4.50 from Paddington"), David Osborn
(adaptation)
Cast: Margaret Rutherford, Arthur Kennedy, Muriel
Pavlow, Thorley Walters, Charles Tingwell, Joan Hickson,
Stringer Davis
JRJ: Ackenthorpe

GUNS OF DARKNESS (1962)
GB. 102 minutes. Black and White
ABP/Cavalcade
Director: Anthony Asquith
Screenplay: John Mortimer, Francis Clifford (novel)
Cast: Leslie Caron, David Niven, David Opatoshu,
Eleanor Summerfield, Ian Hunter
JRJ: Hugo Bryant

A PAIR OF BRIEFS (1962)
GB. 90 minutes. Black and White
Rank
Director: Ralph Thomas
Screenplay: Nicholas Phipps
Cast: Michael Craig, Mary Peach, Brenda De Banzie,
Roland Culver, Liz Fraser, Ron Moody
JRJ: Mr. Justice Haddon

CROOKS ANONYMOUS (1962)
GB. 87 minutes. Black and White
Anglo Amalgamated
Director: Ken Annakin
Screenplay: Henry Blyth & Jack Davies
Cast: Stanley Baxter, Leslie Phillips, Julie Christie,
Wilfred Hyde White, Robertson Hare, Charles Lloyd
Pack
JRJ: Sir Harvey Russelrod

LE REPOS DU GUERRIER (1962)
aka Love on a Pillow (US)
France/Italy. 102 minutes. Colour
Francos Film/Incei Film
Director: Roger Vadim
Screenplay: Roger Vadim
Cast: Brigitte Bardot, Robert Hossein, Jean-Marc Bory,
Michel Serrault, Jacqueline Porel
JRJ: Katov

DAS FEUERSCHIFF (1962)
West Germany. 84 minutes. Black and White
Director: Ladislao Vajda
Screenplay: Curt Siodmak
Cast: Dieter Borsche, Helmut Wildt, Michael Hinz,
Pinkas Braun
JRJ: Kapitän Freytag

THE FAST LADY (1962)
GB. 95 minutes. Colour
Rank/Independent Artists
Director: Ken Annakin
Screenplay: Henry Blyth, Jack Davies, Keble Howard
(story)
Cast: Stanley Baxter, Leslie Phillips, Julie Christie, Dick
Emery
JRJ: Charles Chingford

DR CRIPPEN (1962)
GB. 98 minutes. Black and White
ABP/John Clein
Director: Robert Lynn
Screenplay:Leigh Vance
Cast: Donald Pleasance, Coral Browne, Samantha Eggar,
Donald Wolfit
JRJ: Captain McKenzie

MYSTERY SUBMARINE (1963)
GB. 92 minutes. Black and White
Bertram Ostrer/British Lion
Director: C. M Pennington-Richards
Screenplay:
Cast: Edward Judd, Laurence Payne, Joachim
Fuchsberger, Arthur O'Sullivan, Albert Lieven, Robert
Flemyng
JRJ: Rear Admiral Rainbird

FATHER CAME TOO! (1963)
GB. 91 minutes. Colour
Rank/Independent Artists
Director: Peter Graham-Scott
Screenplay: Henry Blyth, Jack Davies
Cast: Leslie Phillips, Stanley Baxter, Sally Smith, Ronnie
Barker, Eric Barker, Kenneth Cope
JRJ: Sir Beverley Grant

DOCTOR IN DISTRESS (1963)
GB. 102 minutes. Colour
Rank
Director: Ralph Thomas
Screenplay: Nicholas Phipps, Ronald Scott Thorn,
Richard Gordon (novel)
Cast: Dirk Bogarde, Samantha Eggar, Mylène
Demongeot, Donald Houston, Barbara Murray, Dennis
Price, Amanda Barrie
JRJ: Sir Lancelot Spratt

UP FROM THE BEACH (1965)
US. 98 minutes. Black and White
Twentieth Century Fox
Director: Robert Parrish
Screenplay: Calude Brulé, Howard Clewes, Stanley Mann
Cast: Cliff Robertson, Red Buttons, Irina Demick,
Marius Goring, Slim Pickens, Broderick Crawford
JRJ: British Beachmaster

THOSE MAGNIFICENT MEN IN THEIR FLYING MACHINES, OR HOW I FLEW FROM LONDON TO PARIS IN 25 HOURS 11 MINUTES (1964)
GB. 133 minutes. Colour
Twentieth Century Fox
Director: Ken Annakin
Screenplay: Ken Annakin, Jack Davies
Cast: Sarah Miles, Stuart Whitman, Robert Morley, Eric Sykes, Terry-Thomas, James Fox, Alberto Sordi, Gert Fröbe, Jean-Paul Cassel, Karl Michael Vogler, Irina Demick, Benny Hill, Flora Robson, Sam Wanamaker, Red Skelton, Fred Emney, Cicely Cortneidge, Gordon Jackson, John Le Mesurier, Tony Hancock, William Rushton
JRJ: Narrator

THE FACE OF FU MANCHU (1965)
GB/West Germany. 89 minutes. Colour
Hallam Productions/Constantin-Film
Director: Don Sharp
Screenplay: Harry Alan Towers
Cast: Christopher Lee, Nigel Green, Howard Marion-Crawford, Tsai Chin, Walter Rilla
JRJ: Sir Charles/Direktor Fortescu

YOU MUST BE JOKING! (1965)
GB. 99 minutes. Black and White
Columbia
Director: Michael Winner
Screenplay: Alan Hackney (and story), Michael Winner (story)
Cast: Michael Callan, Lionel Jeffries, Denholm Elliott, Wilfred Hyde White, Bernard Cribbins, Terry-Thomas, Irene Handl
JRJ: Librarian

LANGE BEINE – LANGE FINGER (1966)
aka Long Legs Long Fingers (International: English title)
West Germany. 92 minutes. Colour
Director: Alfred Vohrer
Screenplay: Peter Lambda
Cast: Senta Berger, Joachim Fuchsberger, Martin Held, Hanns Lothar, Irina von Meyerndorff, Helga Sommerfeld
JRJ: Sir Hammond

DOCTOR IN CLOVER (1966)
aka Carnaby M D (USA)
GB. 101 minutes. Colour
Rank
Director: Ralph Thomas
Screenplay: Jack Davies, Richard Gordon (novel)
Cast: Leslie Phillips, Shirley Anne Field, John Fraser, Joan Sims, Arthur Haynes
JRJ: Sir Lancelot Spratt

THE TRYGON FACTOR (1966)
West Germany/GB. 88 minutes. Colour
Rank/Rialto Films
Director: Cyril Frankel
Screenplay: Derry Quinn (and story), Stanley Munro, Edgar Wallace (novel 'Kate Plus Ten')
Cast: Stewart Granger, Susan Hampshire, Robert Morley, Cathleen Nesbit, Brigitte Horney, Sophie Hardy
JRJ: Sir John

HELL IS EMPTY (1966)
GB/Czechoslovakia. 109 minutes. Colour
Rank/Dominion
Director: Bernard Knowles, John Ainsworth
Screenplay: John F. Fowler, Bernard Knowles, John Ainsworth
Cast: Martine Carol, Sheila Burrell, Jess Conrad, Anthony Dawson, Shirley Anne Field
JRJ: Angus McGee

À COEUR JOIE (1967)
aka Two Weeks in September (US)
France/GB. 95 minutes. Colour
Francos-Films/Kenwood Films
Diretor: Serge Bourguignon
Screenplay: Serge Bourguignon, Pascal Jardin, Vahé Katcha
Cast: Brigitte Bardot, Laurent Terzieff, Jean Rochefort, Michael Sarne, Georgina Ward
JRJ: McClintock

HISTOIRES EXTRAODRINARIES (1968)
aka Spirits of the Dead (US)
France/Italy. 120 minutes. Colour
Les Films Marceau/Cocinor/PEA
Directors: Roger Vadim, Frederico Fellini, Louis Malle
Screenplay: Edgar Allan Poe (stories), Roger Vadim & Pascal Cousin, (adaptation, "Metzengerstein") Louis Malle & Clement Biddle Wood (adaptation, "William Wilson"), Federico Fellini & Bernardino Zapponi (adaptation, "Toby Dammit"), Daniel Boulanger (dialogue, "William Wilson" and "Metzengerstein")
Cast: Jane Fonda, Bridgett Bardot, Peter Fonda, Alain Delon, Carla Marlier, Terence Stamp
JRJ: Countess' Advisor ("Metzengerstein")

MAYERLING (1968)
France/GB. 141 minutes. Colour
Winchester-Corona
Director: Terence Young
Screenplay:Terence Young, Claude Anet
Cast: Omar Sharif, Catherine Deneuve, James Mason, Ava Gardner
JRJ: Edward, Prince of Wales

CHITTY CHITTY BANG BANG (1968)
aka Ian Fleming's Chitty Chitty Bang Bang (USA)
GB. 145 minutes. Colour
MGM/UA
Director: Ken Hughes
Screenplay: Roald Dahl, Ken Hughs, Ian Fleming (novel)
Cast: Dick Van Dyke, Sally Anne Howes, Lionel Jeffries,
Gert Fröbe, Anna Quayle, Benny Hill
JRJ: Lord Scrumptious

ZETA ONE
aka The Love Factor (USA)
GB. 84 minutes. Colour
Tigon
Director: Michael Cort
Screenplay: Michael Cort, Alistair McKenzie,
Christopher Neame
Cast: Charles Hawtrey, Robin Hawdon, Dawn Addams,
Lionel Murton, Carol Hawkins, Anna Gaël, Valerie Leon
JRJ: Major Bourden

SOME WILL SOME WON'T (1969)
GB. 90 minutes. Colour
ABP/Transocean
Director: Duncan Wood
Screenplay: Michael Pertwee & Jack Davies (screenplay
'Laughter in Paradise'), Lew Schwarz
Cast: Ronnie Corbett, Thora Hird, Michael Hordern,
Leslie Phillips
JRJ: Sir Charles Robson

DOCTOR IN TROUBLE (1970)
GB. 90 minutes. Colour
Rank
Director: Ralph Thomas
Screenplay: Jack Davies, Richard Gordon (novel)
Cast: Leslie Phillips, Robert Morley, Harry Secombe,
Irene Handl, Joan Sims, Freddie Jones, Graham Stark
JRJ: Sir Lancelot Spratt

MASSACRE OF GLENCOE (1971)
GB. 58 minutes. Black and White
Austin Campbell Films
Director: Austin Campbell
Screenplay: Austin Campbell
Cast: Andrew Crawford, Paul Young, Ian Stewart,
George Morgan, Sandra Clark

Selected Documentaries

CHALLENGE OF THE NORTH (1955)
GB. Colour
Group 3 Productions
Editor: Derek York

SCOTTISH CLANS – Clan McPherson (1966)
GB. 15 minutes. Colour
Mica Film Productions
Dir: Hans Nieter

SCOTTISH CLANS – Clan Fraser of Lovat (1966)
GB. 17 minutes. Colour
Mica Film Productions
Dir: Graham Stewart

THE STORY OF SPRINGFIELDS (1966)
GB. 32 minutes. Colour
Guild Sound and Vision
Dir: Peter Ryde

SPRINGTIME AT SPRINGFIELDS (1968)
GB. 14 minutes. Colour
Guild Sound and Vision
Dir: Peter Ryde

GATHERING OF THE CLANS (1968)
GB. 30 minutes. Colour
Austin Campbell Films
Dir: Austin Campbell

THE FALCON GENTLE (1974)
aka The Lure of the Falcon
GB. 33 minutes. Colour
With Stephen Frank, Toby Bromley, Roger Upton, Jack
Mavrogardato
Dir: Toby Bromley

THE CHALK-STREAM TROUT (1974)
aka The Angler and the Trout
GB. 33 minutes. Colour
Dir: Toby Bromley

INDEX

OTHER GREAT BOOKS FROM TOMAHAWK

SO YOU WANNA BE A DIRECTOR?
by Ken Annakin OBE
Forewords by Mike Leigh and Lord Attenborough
ISBN 10: 0-953 1926-5-2 ISBN 13: 978-0-9531926-5-6
RRP: £8.99 Paperback 301pp

Ken Annakin was one of the greatest international film directors. The last of the
English directors to make it on the international arena (others included Hitchcock
and Lean), this 'no holds barred' autobiography traces Annakin's career from his early
British films through to Hollywood. He has directed, written and produced over fifty
feature films in Africa, India, Malaysia, Scandinavia, China, Europe and America. *So You Wanna Be A
Director?* is an entertaining and witty travelogue, as well as an important document of film history.

*"This really is THE film book par excellence… A joy to read, it delivers the goods in a spry and
unpretentious style that is truly entertaining.* ★★★★★*"*
Howard Maxford, Film Review.

There has never been so vivid a portrait of a jobbing film-maker… A rousing autobiography.
Sight and Sound

PATRICK McGOOHAN – DANGER MAN OR PRISONER?
by Roger Langley
Foreword by Peter Falk
FEATURING OVER 450 RARE AND EXCLUSIVE PHOTOGRAPHS
ISBN 10: 0-9531926-4-4 ISBN 13: 978-0-9531926-4-9
RRP: £19.99 Paperback 340pp

In *Patrick McGoohan: Danger Man or Prisoner?*, Roger Langley unravels the myths,
separating the man from his on-screen creations. McGoohan attracts thousands of
admirers around the globe and this book reveals why! The book details
McGoohan's classic television series *Danger Man* and *The Prisoner*, as well as his extensive cinema career.
You will also find out why McGoohan was top choice for James Bond, and why he turned down the role.

ZULU: WITH SOME GUTS BEHIND IT – THE MAKING OF THE EPIC MOVIE
by Sheldon Hall
Foreword by John Barry OBE
Lavishly illustrated with 400 rare B/W and colour images
ISBN 10: 0-9531926-6-0 ISBN 13: 978-0-9531926-6-3
RRP: £25.00 Hardback 456pp

Written in a lively and accessible style, and lavishly illustrated throughout, *Zulu:
With Some Guts Behind It* is based on three years of original research. Author
Sheldon Hall takes us behind the scenes of Britain's favourite war movie and reveals
for the first time the true story of the making of Zulu.

*A class act from first page to last…..A joy to read, movie books really don't come much
better than this!* ★★★★★
Film Review

The #1 film book of the year!
Cinema Retro Magazine

To order and for all the latest information visit www.tomahawkpress.com